America's first jet was the Bell P-59. It was not a success but the Americans quickly learned the secrets of jet engine design. US National Archives

The German Messerschmitt Me 163 was a rocket powered interceptor meant for taking down Allied bombers. It was tricky to fly and its engine relied on highly volatile fuel but the shape of its wings and tail had a direct influence on postwar aircraft design. US National Archives

The story of Concorde begins during the final dark days of the Second World War. Through necessity, aircraft had undergone rapid development on all sides during the conflict with jet and rocket engines being tested by both the British and Germans simultaneously.

The first jet aircraft to fly was German – Hans von Ohain's Heinkel He 178 on August 27, 1939 – followed by the British effort, Frank Whittle's Gloster E.28/39 on May 15, 1941, and finally the American Bell XP-59 on October 1, 1942.

The Americans had initially lagged behind but caught up quickly using technology developed and then handed over by the British.

Before the war, during the 1930s, even highly specialised racing aircraft struggled to reach speeds in excess of 450mph but with jet and rocket engines such speeds could easily be matched and exceeded.

German rocket powered Messerschmitt 163s regularly topped 600mph and shortly after the end of the war Britain's first production jet fighter, the Gloster Meteor managed it too – setting official world speed records in the process.

As early as 1943 however, the British had been secretly working on another project which would dramatically exceed the flight speed of these early aircraft – the Miles M.52. With little information available on the new German high speed aircraft, it was feared that they might be able to exceed 1000mph and efforts were made to at least match this.

The M.52 utilised flight test data which had identified the relatively broad and graceful shape of aircraft such as the Supermarine Spitfire as one of the main impediments to achieving extreme speeds. Its designers also studied unmanned projectiles to see how they moved through the air at high speed. Therefore the M.52 had very thin very short wings, a cockpit forming a shock cone in the nose to reduce the speed of air entering its jet engine, and a powered all-moving tail.

Britain signed an agreement with the US in 1944 for share aerodynamic test data and the details of the M.52 were duly handed over but nothing was forthcoming in return since the Americans were working on a secret speed project of their own, the Bell X-1, and were unwilling to reveal its existence, even to an ally. The X-1 design later incorporated a powered all-moving tail.

There were further developments in 1945. While the early British and American jets were shaped like traditional fighter aircraft with straight wings, the Germans had carried out research on wing and fuselage shapes which produced dramatically different aerodynamic effects.

The last days of the war had seen German engineers and designers desperately searching for a means of stopping the waves of Allied bombers that regularly flew unopposed at high altitude overhead and rained thousands of tonnes of high explosives down on their cities.

To this end, they drafted radical designs for arrow shaped aircraft, aircraft with broad delta wings, aircraft that were just one gigantic wing and even aircraft with swept forward wings, one of which was built and actually flew as the Junkers Ju 287.

When the war ended, the victorious British, American and Russian allies sent teams into the ruined remains of German aircraft factories and workshops to seek out and capture whatever prototype jet and rocket aircraft they could find, ideally along with the men who designed them and the blueprints they had drafted.

Using this captured research, all three powers embarked on a programme of aircraft development which would have dramatic results. As Britain wound down its military spending after the Second World War, the M.52, which had once seemed so promising, was cancelled as a piloted jet aircraft but resurrected in miniature as a 1:3 scale rocket powered remote controlled test drone that was to be air launched from a de

Fast, faster, fastest!

The desire to achieve ever greater speeds has been a part of aviation since its earliest days.

Wilbur Wright's first flight in the Wright Flyer at Kitty Hawk, North Carolina, in 1903, hit a top speed of just over 6mph. Wright's Wright Flyer III was still only managing 37mph two years later.

The air speed record was broken four times in 1909, three more times in 1910, five times in 1911 and seven times in 1912. By February 8, 1920, it stood at 171mph. By 1930 it was 357.7mph – a record having been set by the Supermarine S.6 seaplane, which would eventually evolve into the Supermarine Spitfire. The last record set before the onset of the Second World War was achieved by German test pilot Fritz Wendel flying a Messerschmitt 209 – a highly specialised racer which, despite its name, had very little in common with the Messerschmitt's successful Bf 109.

The North American F-86 Sabre jet fighter had beaten the rocket powered Bell X-1 by the end of the 1940s to clock up 670.84mph and the end of the 1950s saw another American fighter, the Convair F-106 Delta Dart, holding the title with an impressive 1525.9mph.

By the end of the 1960s the desperate dash to achieve higher and higher speeds had slowed with huge development costs inhibiting progress. The last non-rocket powered record of the decade, 2070.1mph, was set in 1965 by Robert L Stephens and Daniel Andre in a Lockheed YF-12A – a prototype aircraft from the same programme that would result in the fastest non-rocket powered manned aircraft ever.

The last and current record holder is the Lockheed SR-71 Blackbird, which clocked up a speed of 2193.2mph on July 28, 1976. With the aid of a rocket engine, pilot William 'Pete' Knight managed to hit 4519mph or Mach 6.72 in the X-15 in 1967 and an unmanned ramjet/scramjet, the X-43A, hit 10,461mph or Mach 8.4 in 2005.

The fastest man has ever travelled is on board the Space Shuttle, which orbits at a speed of 17,500mph.

Concorde never quite managed to achieve the world records that its designers had hoped for – being consistently pipped to the post by the Russian copycat Tu-144. Concorde first went supersonic on October 1, 1969. The Russians had managed it on June 5 of the same year. Concorde exceeded Mach 2 on November 4, 1970. The Tu-144 had done it on May 26. And to add insult to injury, the Tu-144 still holds the world record for fastest airliner at 1600mph or Mach 2.4.

> **WHEN THE WAR ENDED, THE VICTORIOUS BRITISH, AMERICAN AND RUSSIAN ALLIES SENT TEAMS INTO THE RUINED REMAINS OF GERMAN AIRCRAFT FACTORIES AND WORKSHOPS TO SEEK OUT AND CAPTURE WHATEVER PROTOTYPE JET AND ROCKET AIRCRAFT THEY COULD FIND**

An artist's impression of the Miles M.52, Britain's wartime attempt to create a superfast aerial testbed. Its design incorporated cutting edge innovations but it was cancelled as a full scale manned project in 1946 only to be resurrected in scale model form in 1947. Crown Copyright

Havilland Mosquito aircraft at high altitude where thinner air would enable greater speeds to be achieved.

Britain's research continued with the de Havilland DH.108 Swallow test aircraft. This was based on a Vampire jet fighter, Britain's second to fly before the end of the war, but incorporated elements of the Me 163 – particularly its tailless swept wing shape. Three prototypes were built and the first was used by de Havilland test pilot Geoffrey de Havilland Jr in a series of flights in May 1946 to gather information about the low speed handling characteristics of a swept wing.

The second prototype, fitted with a more powerful jet engine, began flights in June but during a run to see how it handled at high speed on September 27, a buildup of shockwaves around the aircraft at Mach 0.9 caused uncontrollable oscillations and a shock stall. The subsequent tremendous pressure placed on the airframe caused the wings to break off at their roots and fold backwards. de Havilland suffered a broken neck as his head whipped to one side and struck the aircraft's canopy and died during the crash after it dived from 10,000ft into the Thames Estuary.

In October the following year, the first test of the miniature M.52 took place but shortly after it was released the little aircraft's Armstrong Siddeley Beta rocket engine, based on a German design from the Second World War, exploded. Just a few days later, on October 14, 1947, American test pilot Chuck Yeager became the first man to break the sound barrier – travelling at over 800mph, Mach 1.06, in a rocket powered bullet shaped Bell X1.

Concorde – 10 years on

Foreword by Captain Mike Bannister, Chief Concorde Pilot, British Airways

"That's one small step for a man, one giant leap for mankind".We all relate to these resonating words from Neil Armstrong, spoken as he took the very first step on the moon's surface. It was July 21, 1969, a momentous day in human advancement and achievement; memorable as a huge demonstration of our ability to design, build and operate the most sophisticated pieces of machinery and to attain our dreams.

Yet Apollo 11's moon landing had been preceded three months earlier by another amazing feat. The first flight of Concorde. I have always thought that there was some fated link between the two events – a belief brought to reality when I met Neil Armstrong on November 3, 2006.

He was awarded the Guild of Air Pilots and Air Navigators Award of Honour which is presented on rare occasions "to individuals who have made an outstanding lifetime contribution to aviation".

As a past master of the guild I was honoured to dine with him and to chat at length about all things aeronautical. When the conversation turned to Concorde I was astounded to hear him freely say that "the Concorde Project was just as great a technical achievement as putting me on the moon".

In agreeing with him I immediately asked myself why?

Was it flying on the edge of space, where the sky got darker and you could see the curvature of the earth? Was it travelling faster than the earth rotates? Was it arriving before you've left? Was it buying back time? 2160kph, 1350mph, 22½ miles a minute, a mile in less than 2¾ seconds? Was it being in a lounge suit when all around you were in spacesuits? Yes, it was all of these – and so much more.

Like Concorde, Apollo 11 first flew in 1969. However the Apollo programme finished in 1972, Concorde flew on until 2003. The Apollo programme flew just 24 astronauts to the moon (and only half of them landed!), British Airways Concorde carried 2,500,000 passengers to over 250 destinations worldwide – 76 of those in the US. The Apollo programme cost the US taxpayer $25 billion ($100 billion in today's money), Concorde made over £500 million profit for British Airways.

The Apollo programme gave us technologies that are still used in everyday life – scratch resistant lenses, athletic shoes, cordless power tools. Concorde gave us aviation advances used around the world today – fly by wire controls, carbon fibre brakes, and computerised engine control.

And yet it's not all of that we remember when we look back over the 10 years since Concorde last flew. It's the beauty of it. A beauty that appeals to one side of our brains while the technology appeals to the other. The psychologists tell us that's why we always looked up as Concorde flew over. Of course, it could have been the noise!

Detractors will always find something to complain about. Noise, cost, exclusivity. Concorde was less noisy than its contemporaries, the 707 and the VC10. It made lots and lots of operating profit and only around 10% of those who flew on Concorde could be described as the 'rich and famous'. For so many it was the trip of a lifetime.

So, looking back to the day when I flew the last ever Concorde scheduled flight and landed back at Heathrow on October 24, 2003, what are the most enduring memories 10 years on? An aircraft that was a joy to fly – more like a thoroughbred racehorse than a riding school hack? An aircraft that was a technically superb as the Apollo missions? An aircraft that paved the way for much that we use in aviation today? Yes, these memories are there, but not at the forefront of my mind.

Concorde was born from dreams, built with vision and operated with pride. The common factor among all of that are the people. It's the people that made Concorde special; the designers, the manufacturers, the flight crews, the cabin crews, the engineers, the loaders, the ramp staff, the planners, the support staff, the passengers and, most of all, the public. Those that just looked up and dreamed. Those that remember, 10 years on as they take eight hours to cross the Atlantic rather than just three hours, 20 minutes, just how amazing this aircraft was.

Enjoy looking back on her. It will be a long time before we see her like again.

**Mike Bannister
London, June 2013**

Concorde

Supersonic Speedbird – the full story

G-BOAF

Contents

Author:
Bernard Bale

Editor:
Dan Sharp

Designers:
Libby Fincham, Justin Blackamore

Reprographics:
Jonathan Schofield, Simon Duncan

Group production editor:
Tim Hartley

Production manager:
Craig Lamb

Marketing manager:
Charlotte Park

Publisher:
Dan Savage

Commercial director:
Nigel Hole

Managing director:
Brian Hill

Published by:
Mortons Media Group Ltd,
Media Centre,
Morton Way, Horncastle,
Lincolnshire LN9 6JR
Tel: 01507 529529

Printed by:
William Gibbons and Sons,
Wolverhampton

Credits:
All photographs courtesy PA Images
unless otherwise stated.
Main cover photograph by
Steve Flint via Air Team Images
www.airteamimages.com
Back cover photograph by
Tim Callaway

ISBN 978-1-909128-07-1

Going supersonic

The research that made Concorde possible

Concorde was the embodiment of decades of research and aircraft design development. The dream of supersonic flight began during the Second World War when ever more powerful and technologically advanced military aircraft began to experience unforeseen problems the faster they went...

Britain's jet age starts here. Frank Whittle's revolutionary Gloster E.28/39 was the nation's first jet aircraft to take flight. Crown Copyright

The Bell X-1 broke the sound barrier for the first time with test pilot Chuck Yeager at the controls. NASA

The X-1 had initially been tested as an unpowered glider in early 1946 before being fitted with its Reaction Motors XLR-11 rocket engine. Numerous successful flights took place between September 1946 and June 1947 when the military took direct control of the project off Bell Aircraft and put Yeager at the controls. His record breaking flight began with an air-launch from the belly of a modified B-29 Superfortress and ended with an unpowered glide down on to a dry lake bed. Word of this feat quickly got out and the Americans were suddenly leading the world in supersonic aircraft development. Britain only caught up in September 1948 when test pilot John Derry took a modified DH.108 through the sound barrier during a dive.

While the Swallow experiments continued. The world's first jet airliner, the de Havilland Comet, took flight on July 27, 1949. The Comet was another product of the war years although it was certainly never intended as a military machine. Showing remarkable foresight, the British government had laid plans for this pioneering passenger transport as early as March 1943. It had determined that what the nation would really need once victory had been achieved – even though D-Day was still over a year away, let alone VE Day – was a pressurised aircraft capable of flying across the Atlantic to America at a speed greater than 400mph carrying a payload of at least one ton. At the insistence of Geoffrey de Havilland, de Havilland company founder and father of the ill-fated DH.108 test pilot of the same name, it was

Test pilot Chuck Yeager with the Bell X-1 he named after his wife – Glamorous Glennis.

even specified that the transport should be jet powered. The contract to build it went, unsurprisingly, to de Havilland.

It was initially envisioned that the DH.106 would be small, with perhaps six seats. This was quickly revised to 24 seats and then 36. British Airways forerunner the British Overseas Airways Corporation (BOAC), having seen the plans, submitted a tentative order for 25 aircraft but later got cold feet and revised the total down to just 10.

As research data and outlandish wartime designs were picked through and assessed,

the de Havilland design team considered everything from delta wings to canards but eventually settled on something a little more conventional, particularly after the problems experienced by the firm's own DH.108 programme. The DH.106 that emerged from the drawing board stage therefore had swept wings but an ordinary looking tail. Inside the fuselage, the 36 seats were arranged in nine rows of four seats with a single extremely narrow aisle down the middle.

When the DH.106 was originally conceived, it was to have been fitted with de

The Fairey Delta 2. It broke the world air speed record and held it for more than a year. It had a droopable nose which would become a standard feature on supersonic airliner designs worldwide.

Havilland's own Goblin jet engines but this was then changed to four Rolls-Royce Avons, two on either side where the wings joined the fuselage. Delays then forced a second switch, this time to de Havilland's new Ghost engine. The DH.106 was named Comet in December 1947 and was on course for delivery to the airline firms that were eagerly awaiting it by 1952.

Stress testing of fuselage sections took place during 1948 using a decompression chamber and then a water tank, since the Comet had yet to take flight. Ground tests and the first flight of the prototype, registered G-ALVG, followed at Hatfield Aerodrome.

The same aircraft flew at the 1949 Farnborough Air Show and a second prototype, G-ALZK, was rolled out in July 1950. Airlines around the world were now beginning to sit up and take notice, with Australian Qantas even sending its own technical team over to Britain to assess the Comet. The production version appeared in January 1951.

The earliest BOAC examples had reclining seats with extra legroom and all Comets had large square windows offering an unparalled view for passengers. There were separate gents' and ladies' toilets in addition to air conditioning, a galley for serving hot food and drinks, life vests under every seat and lift rafts in the wings. In the cockpit there were powered dual controls for the pilot and co-pilot and in later versions the aircraft's nose housed a powerful radar. The Comet was faster and quieter than most other airliners and it

could soar above bad weather that others had to fly through.

The Comet's fuselage was made from advanced alloys using both rivets and chemical bonding techniques which had not been seen before in civil aviation but the location of its cargo bay doors, underneath the plane's body rather than on either side of it, made life difficult for baggage handlers. Despite this minor difficulty, the Comet was a hit. The Queen, Queen Mother and Princess flew on board one in June 1953 with Geoffrey de Havilland and his wife and during its first year the aircraft carried 30,000 passengers. It was soon being operated not only by BOAC but also French airlines Air France and Union Aéromaritime de Transport. Orders came flooding in from Japan Airlines, Air India, British Commonwealth Pacific Airlines, Linea Aeropostal Venezolana, Panair do Brasil, Capital Airlines, National Airlines and even Pan Am. Qantas still held off however.

The first sign of trouble came on October 6, 1952. A BOAC Comet struggled to take off at Rome and ended up rolling right off the end of the runway. A second Comet incident occurred on March 3, 1953, when a Canadian Pacific Airlines example also struggled to get airborne in Pakistan and instead crashed into a canal killing its six passengers and five crew. Pilot error was blamed in both cases although later investigation resulted in de Havilland making some alterations to the Comet's wing shape. Worse was to come. On May 2, 1953, a BOAC Comet crashed during a

thunderstorm in India, killing all 43 of its passengers and crew. This time several witnesses reported seeing the burning Comet, minus its wings, crashing into the ocean. Concerns were raised about the aircraft's structural safety but again pilot error was blamed, combined with the effects of the storm. Henceforth, Comets would need to have weather radar and mechanical changes to prevent pilots from overstressing the aircraft during extreme conditions.

The accidents continued however. Another Comet broke up in mid-air in Italy on January 10, 1954, killing 35. The inquiry focused on six possible causes – control flutter, metal fatigue of the wing structure, failure of the flight control systems, failure of the passenger compartment's square windows, a fire or engine trouble. Fire was deemed the most likely cause and Comets underwent further changes to safeguard against it. Flights resumed on March 23, 1954, but just over two weeks later, on April 8, yet another Comet crashed. The entire fleet was grounded and production at Hatfield was halted.

A huge water tank was constructed to test the effects of stress on a complete Comet fuselage for the first time and the results were conclusive – it was the windows. Stress accumulated at the corners of those big square windows and after 3057 'flights' the airframe itself tore open. In the air, this would have caused catastrophic structural failure. The riveting technique used in the Comet was also found to be at fault but henceforth all commercial airliners

The prototype for the incredible English Electric Lightning jet fighter, the P.1, was the first British aircraft to achieve speeds greater than Mach 2. The one pictured here was the first P.1 made.

ABOVE: High speed pioneer Peter Twiss who piloted the Fairey Delta 2 on its record breaking run.

LEFT: An early de Havilland Comet airliner with square windows sits beside one of the three DH.108s. This one, VW120, was flown past the sound barrier by test pilot John Derry in 1948.

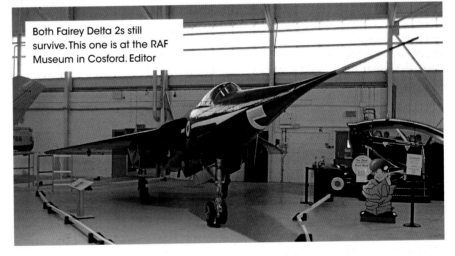

Both Fairey Delta 2s still survive. This one is at the RAF Museum in Cosford. Editor

have had round windows. Comet itself was re-engineered and re-entered service, eventually being extensively modified to become the RAF Nimrod which remained in operation until 2011 – 60 years after the Comet's first flight.

While the Comet was getting back on its feet in the form of the Comet 2 and the rest of the world was catching up in the race to create the best commercial airliner, British engineers were completing work on what would become one of the nation's most famous and successful supersonic aircraft – the English Electric Lightning. All the data so far gathered from the M.52, DH.108 and other tests was brought together in the form of the Lightning's prototype, the English Electric P.1. Work was also being carried out on the aircraft that would form Britain's nuclear deterrent – the Vulcan, Victor and Valiant bombers and subsonic jet fighter aircraft such as the Supermarine Swift.

The P.1 had a gaping triangular jet intake instead of a nose and a notched delta wing and it underwent extensive testing, only taking flight for the first time at RAF Boscombe Down on August 4, 1954. It was powered by a pair of Armstrong Siddeley Sapphire engines fitted one on top of the other in its narrow fuselage before these were replaced by the incredibly powerful Rolls-Royce Avon. The P.1B became the first British aircraft to hit Mach 2 on November 25, 1958. Shortly after the P.1's first flight, another groundbreaking British jet made its debut – the experimental Fairey Delta 2. Designed as a pure high speed research

aircraft, not only did it have a Rolls-Royce Avon, it also sported delta wings and another feature previously unseen in aviation – the droop snoot. This innovation came about because the aircraft needed to be straight as an arrow for maximum streamlining during supersonic flight but the pilot also needed to be able to see ahead while taxiing, taking off and landing. The solution was to give the Delta 2 a hinged nose that could drop down by 10° to provide the pilot with extra visibility.

Several attempts were made to break the world air speed record with the Delta 2 in 1956. By now it was held by an American fighter aircraft, the North American F-100C Super Sabre, at 822.1mph. After seven unsuccessful runs – unsuccessful because the recording equipment could not be made

to accurately gauge the Delta 2's phenomenal speed, the record was finally broken on March 10, 1956, by pilot Peter Twiss. He beat the American record by more than 300mph at a speed of 1132mph. It was the first time an aircraft had gone faster than 1000mph in level flight.

Incredibly, the record stood for more than a year before being beaten on December 12, 1957, by an American McDonnell F-101A Voodoo. Now though, the actual numbers were almost irrelevant. Ever faster supersonic speeds were within reach and the eyes of the world focused on the Fairey Delta 2 with its remarkable nose and delta wing. It didn't take too much imagination to see how these might be applied to civilian air transport. It was just a question of who would get there first.

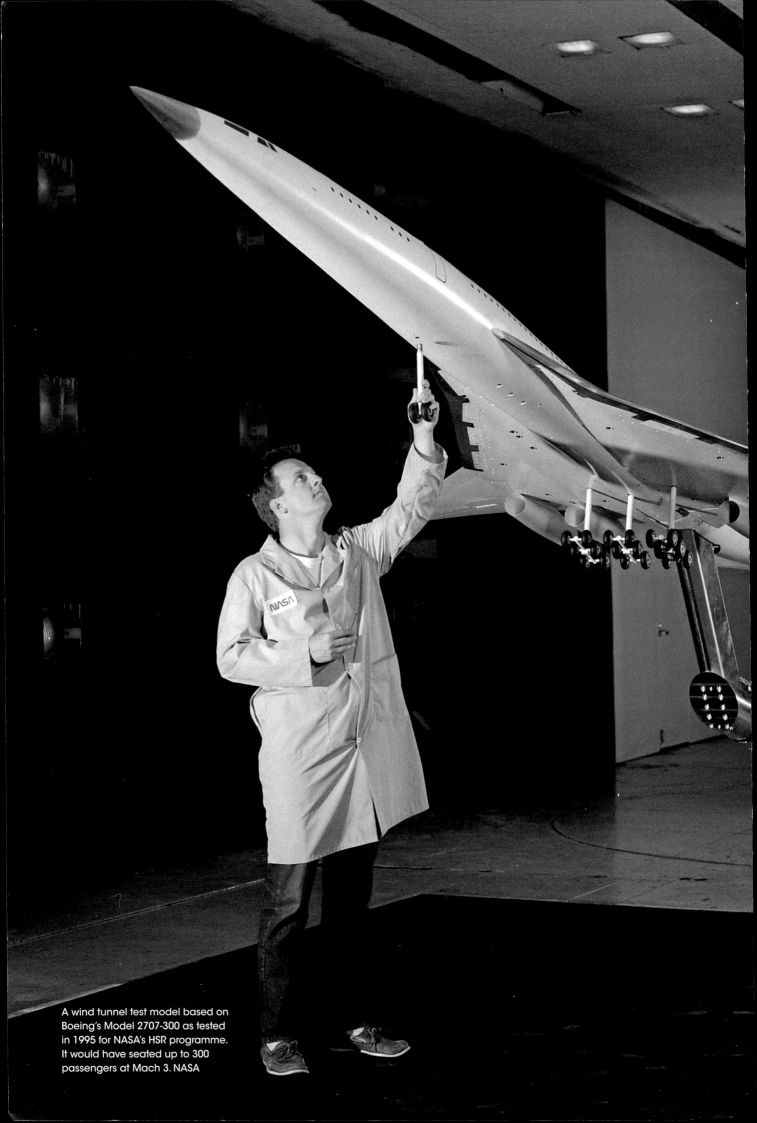

A wind tunnel test model based on Boeing's Model 2707-300 as tested in 1995 for NASA's HSR programme. It would have seated up to 300 passengers at Mach 3. NASA

CHAPTER TWO

Airliner of the future

Concorde, Concordski and the SST race

The early development of Concorde saw its British and French designers and engineers competing first against one another and then together against the Americans. But there was also a rank outsider waiting in the wings that was perhaps the most dangerous competitor of all…

When Britain's Fairey Delta 2 went supersonic in 1956, topping 1000mph for the first time and breaking the world air speed record by more than 300mph the three other world superpowers sat up and took notice.

America, France and the USSR now knew that the technology existed to propel a manned aircraft at previously undreamt of speeds. Missiles were already beginning to make such an innovation redundant for military purposes but as the new age of civil transport dawned and demand for ever faster and more comfortable airliners grew fresh possibilities emerged.

Less than eight months later, the first meeting of Britain's Supersonic Transport Aircraft Committee (STAC) took place at Farnborough. The nation's great hope for the civil transport market, the de Havilland Comet was turning into a disaster and the Americans were rapidly gaining the initiative with the Boeing 367-80 or 'Dash 80' – the prototype form of the Boeing 707. The production version entered service with Pan American World Airways in October 1958. Douglas's DC-8 and Convair's 880 joined it in carrying fare paying passengers in 1959,

along with the French competitor, the Sud Aviation Caravelle.

Back in 1956, the members of STAC knew something had to be done, and quickly, if Britain was to come out fighting against these foreign designs. Under its auspices three firms, Bristol, Handley Page and Hawker Siddeley, began working on proposals for the next generation of jet airliners which would deliver far greater speed and comfort than had been possible with the troubled Comet.

At the same time, Barnes Wallis, inventor of the famous 'bouncing bomb' used by 617 Squadron during the Dams Raid in 1943, was developing a Government-backed project initially codenamed Wild Goose and later Swallow. The former involved designs for a high speed military machine but the latter was intended to produce an airliner that would take passengers on a nonstop flight from London to Sydney, Australia, in under 10 hours. A 6ft model of Swallow, a rocket powered design that blended its fuselage with a set of swing-wings, managed to hit speeds of up to Mach 2.5 but when the Government pulled the plug on it in 1957, Wallis took the idea to the Americans.

The Sud Aviation Caravelle was France's first successful jet airliner and after its introduction the firm began to look at designs for a supersonic successor.

He'd hoped for funding in the form of a grant but instead the Americans simply took it as a reminder of the potential of swing-wing designs – something they had already explored for themselves with the relatively small Bell X-5 and Grumman XF10F Jaguar. Having watched Wallis demonstrate what could happen if you married a swing-wing with a much larger airframe, the Americans began the TFX (Tactical Fighter Experimental) programme, resulting eventually in the creation of the General Dynamics F-111. Vickers, which had been running the Swallow programme, even considered suing the Americans but this plan was ultimately dropped.

Over in the US itself, Boeing had already conducted preliminary studies the creation of a supersonic transport (SST) in 1952 but dismissed the idea as too costly and impractical. Two years later, the American government issued a requirement for a manned bomber capable of flying to the USSR which would be ready to replace the B-52 by 1965. In 1955 this rather vague requirement was brought into sharper focus with a requirement for a bomber which, while it had the same

range requirement, also had to fly faster than Mach 2 at an altitude of 60,000ft and above.

In 1956, the first test flight of the delta-winged Convair B-58 Hustler took place. The Hustler would go on to become the world's first Mach 2 bomber but its development programme was fraught with difficulties. Convair struggled with a tight time schedule imposed on it by the US Air Force and five of the first 20 Hustlers built were lost in accidents. Many felt that the B-58 had flown before it was ready and plans were already in motion for a replacement.

Like Convair, Boeing and North American had been working towards the US government's bomber requirement and each had come up with a long slender delta winged design. The government placed both designs in competition in 1957 and North American won. While it began work on what would become the XB-70 Valkyrie bomber, Boeing took the bomber designs it had developed and reimagined them as civilian airliners. Its Dash-80 was already looking extremely promising and it established a team to examine the potential of SST designs in detail in 1958.

THE TOUGH GET GOING

While the Americans were struggling with their faster than sound bomber designs and the French were beginning to consider the next step beyond the successful Caravelle airliner, the British STAC had not been idle. Bristol in particular had developed a series of concepts it called Type 198 which all involved a pointed nose, a long fuselage and delta wings combined with a set of high-powered engines. Chief designer Archibald Russell was particularly fascinated by the possibilities of a narrow delta wing shape combined with a stainless steel alloy which would be able to withstand the incredible heat of speeds greater than Mach 2. Tests had demonstrated that aluminium, the usual material of choice for aircraft construction, couldn't stand much more than Mach 2.2 on a regular basis. Russell therefore set about working on a version of Type 198 that could be made from steel – Type 213.

The members of STAC reported in March 1959 that the commercial market could support two supersonic machines – one that could manage Mach 1.2 for medium range flights with fewer than 100 passengers and one that could do Mach 2 for long haul trips

ABOVE: Convair's B-58 Hustler was America's first Mach 2 capable bomber. Aspects of its design were incorporated into the later XB-70 Mach 3 bomber which itself formed the basis of North American's entry into the SST race, the NAC-60. USAF Museum

ABOVE RIGHT: Pioneering engineer Barnes Wallis with a model of his swing-wing Vickers Swallow aircraft. He took the design to the US with hopes of securing grant funding to develop it. Instead, the Americans developed the idea without him. Boeing used it for its first supersonic transport designs.

RIGHT: The XB-70 Valkyrie bomber. It never went into serial production but it helped to develop the technology which, it was hoped, would help an American SST beat Concorde. USAF Museum

> CHIEF DESIGNER ARCHIBALD RUSSELL WAS PARTICULARLY FASCINATED BY THE POSSIBILITIES OF A NARROW DELTA WING SHAPE COMBINED WITH A STAINLESS STEEL ALLOY WHICH WOULD BE ABLE TO WITHSTAND THE INCREDIBLE HEAT OF SPEEDS GREATER THAN MACH 2.

with 150. Actually paying for the development of such aircraft at the height of the Cold War was another matter however. The Government of the day, Harold Macmillan's Conservatives, decided that only one aircraft would be necessary and put the medium range proposal on hold to concentrate on the Mach 2 long range machine. The two competing designs were from what was formerly Bristol, it having merged with several other firms to form the British Aircraft Corporation (BAC) on January 1, 1960, and Hawker Siddeley. The BAC design was the preferred option. As development work continued a smaller version of Type 198 with just 100 seats, Type 223, was drawn up and was quickly selected as preferable to the

Type 198. Work also began on rebuilding one of the two Fairey Delta 2s, WG774, as a flying testbed for SST technology including ogee-ogive wings – a similar smooth flowing double curve to that later seen on Concorde.

Bristol and then BAC had hoped that a revolution in thinly rolled steel aircraft construction would result in a material that could cope with speeds of Mach 2.5 and possibly even Mach 3 and above. A test aircraft, the Bristol Type 188, had been in development since 1953 but had been repeatedly been delayed by the engine difficulties by the sheer complexity of making a steel body material that would work. When it eventually did fly in 1962, it was a huge disappointment and the steel body never

performed in the way it was hoped that it would. Thereafter all attempts to create Britain's SST from steel, and have it fly faster than Mach 2.2, were quietly dropped.

Thought was also being given to the Type 223's engine. The most suitable option was the outstandingly powerful and already proven Bristol Olympus which, by 1960, had been powering Avro Vulcan bombers for five years. The Vulcan versions produced around 11,000lb-ft of thrust apiece but development had continued since then and a significantly more powerful version had been put into production for the TSR.2 supersonic bomber project. This was the Olympus 320. It offered 22,000lb-ft of thrust or 30,610lb-ft with an afterburner fitted and it was ideal.

THE FULL FAT SSTS

Having already got its B-58 Hustler into service, Convair felt it was well placed in 1960 to offer up a modified version as America's first SST. The proposal, dubbed Model 58-9, involved a three phased approach. First, a military B-58 would fly commercial routes and gather data on how much faster they could be flown by a supersonic machine.

Assuming the numbers looked good, a second phase would involve the Hustler's ginormous underslung fuel pod being replaced with a detachable cabin featuring doors, windows, five seats and an air conditioning system. This would test the effects of supersonic travel on passengers. All being well, a new SST would be designed based directly upon the B-58 layout but with 52 seats inside a greatly lengthened fuselage. Unfortunately official interest and, more importantly, funding from the American Government was still lacking and the concept was never taken forward.

Boeing's SST team had also come up with a set of SST designs by 1960 under the catchall designation Model 733 but it faced the same problems as Convair. Most of Boeing's futuristic looking designs had delta wings but among them was a proposal for a swing-wing passenger aircraft. With a little work, this became a military machine suitable for the TFX programme announced by the US government in 1961. Both the USAF and the US Navy wanted a heavy supersonic fighter that could carry a substantial payload over long distances. Both also agreed that it should feature a swing-wing.

Bids for the TFX contract were put forward by Boeing, General Dynamics, Lockheed, North American, Republic and McDonnell and the first two were taken through to a second round. The air force liked Model 733 but the navy didn't much like either of them. Eventually the General Dynamics design won, becoming the F-111 Aardvark for the USAF and the F-111B for the navy. The latter was a costly failure and was replaced by the F-14 Tomcat. This, however, was small comfort to Boeing in December 1962 when it ultimately lost the contract.

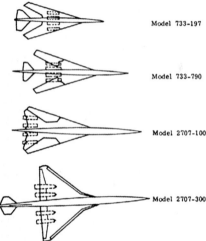

Model 733-197

Model 733-790

Model 2707-100

Model 2707-300

ABOVE: Flying faster than Mach 2 was a hazardous activity in the 1960s. The technology was still in its infancy, as shown by this XB-70. The brown patches on its fuselage are where the sheer heat generated by its speed has burned its paint off. The other aircraft is a B-58. USAF Museum

LEFT: The various stages of the Boeing SST design process – from the compact 733-197 to the much larger 733-790, the bloated and unworkable 2707-100 and the final, cancelled, 2707-300. NASA

BELOW: The failed Lockheed SST bid in two forms – early and late versions of the CL-873. The design on the right would go forward and later be rechristened the L-2000. NASA

France's Sud Aviation revealed its plans to follow up the now-successful Caravelle jet airliner with an SST dubbed the Super-Caravelle. The initial designs, showcased in 1961, were for an aircraft remarkably similar to the Bristol Type 223 with a long thin fuselage and curved delta wings. It was, however, much smaller – designed to take just 70 passengers. Furthermore, the French had more modest aspirations for its speed and range since they lacked anything close to the power output of the Olympus.

This revelation intrigued the British, who were beginning to baulk at the ongoing

costs associated with the development of a faster than sound passenger plane. Talks were soon opened with the French and on November 29, 1962, a formal agreement was signed which marked the beginning of the Concorde project. The French had wanted two aircraft to be produced in partnership – a smaller medium range Super-Caravelle style aircraft and a larger longer range machine based on the Type 223. It was soon realised however that airlines had little interest in the smaller type and work on it was discontinued to focus all efforts on what would become Concorde.

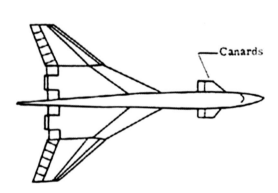

(a) Lockheed CL-823.

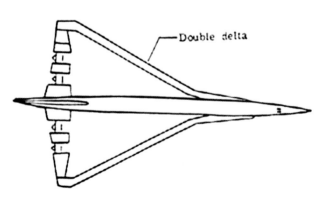

(b) Lockheed double delta.

The Bell X-5 was one of the earliest aircraft to used swing-wings – originally a key feature of America's chosen Concorde challenger. NASA

King of the swingers

America's main competitor in the race to create the first supersonic transport aircraft, the Boeing 733, was intended to have wings which could swing forwards for greater lift at low speeds and swing back to improve aerodynamic efficiency when travelling fast.

Inventive British engineer Barnes Wallis had previously demonstrated his idea for a swing-wing airliner to the Americans and was somewhat nonplussed when the yanks not only declined to financially support his project but then started drawing up designs of their own for large aircraft with what he regarded as his idea incorporated into them.

While the Wallis's team at British manufacturer Vickers thought that the Americans had infringed on their patents as embodied by Swallow, particularly the positioning of the swing-wing pivot, the Americans actually went back to their own research of the early 1950s.

At the end of the Second World War, among the technology captured from the Germans was an advanced jet fighter type known as the Messerschmitt P.1101. Work on building the prototype had almost been completed and the Americans shipped it back home with the associated blueprints and designs.

These were used to create the Bell X-5 in 1951. It not only looked like the P.1101, it also incorporated a more developed version of its pioneering swing-wing design. The X-5 underwent numerous tests and while the wing design, which could be altered to 20°, 40° and 60° angles in flight, was interesting, it was competing against dozens of other designs being trialled by the Americans at the time and by 1955 interest had well and truly been lost.

Another swing-wing, this time the US Navy's Grumman XF10F, was tested in 1951-52 but the firm's engineers struggled to make it work. There were problems with the XF10F's Westinghouse XJ-40 engine and its tail was problematic. After just 32 flights the Jaguar was dropped in 1953.

This might have been the end of the story, had it not been for Wallis who, unaware of America's earlier experiments, believed he had hit upon something truly unique. Having seen his design in action, the Americans were abruptly reawakened to the potential of swinging wings and used the idea to great effect in the F-111 and later the F-14 Tomcat. These in turn inspired a whole generation of 'variable geometry' aircraft such as the Russian MiG-23/-27 Flogger, Sukhoi Su-17/-20/-22 and Su-24, Dassault's aborted Mirage G and the Panavia Tornado.

Salvation, though, seemed to come in the form of the British-French agreement signed a month earlier. When he took office in early 1962, President John F Kennedy asked the US Federal Aviation Authority (FAA) to write him a report on the nation's future civil aviation goals. The man who wrote that report, Najeeb Halaby, suggested that creating an SST would be in America's best interests. He was largely ignored. Three days after the announcement of the British-French deal, he wrote to Kennedy and told him that the Europeans were stealing a march on America, and that if no action was taken thousands of American jobs would be put at risk. The following May, Pan Am revealed that was seriously considering its own Concorde fleet and a month later Kennedy announced the National Supersonic Transport programme.

Invitations to submit designs were sent to Boeing, Lockheed and North American. Engine manufacturers were also notified and the race was on. This was exactly what Boeing had been hoping for and it was able to bring out its Model 733 as Model 733-197 almost immediately, which at this stage looked something like a modern day Rockwell B-1 Lancer bomber. It was envisioned that the supersonic swing-wing transport would be able to comfortably accommodate between 150 and 220 passengers depending on how far the fuselage could be lengthened.

Lockheed's proposal, the CL-823, later known as the L-2000, looked very much like a supersized Concorde – the same only bigger. It would be 273ft long compared to Concorde's 202ft. Its wingspan was 116ft compared to 84ft, it would travel at Mach 3, rather than Mach 2, it would carry 200 passengers rather than a meagre 100 and it would fly at 76,500ft rather than 60,000ft. The nose would droop just like Concorde's and it would have Pratt & Whitney J58 engines – similar to those Lockheed was already planning to use on its SR-71 Blackbird.

The design put forward by North American, the NAC-60, embodied the knowledge and technology it had accumulated during the XB-70 Valkyrie programme. It certainly looked superficially similar but it differed substantially in detail. Rather than the Valkyrie's double tailfins it had just one in the centre and while the large canards near the cockpit made the jump from one design to the other, the six turbofan engines clustered together beneath the rear of the aircraft were ditched in favour of two pods of two engines each, one slung beneath each wing. Its fuselage would contain enough seats for up to 187 passengers.

WHAT KILLED THE GIANTS?

The three main contenders for the American SST crown were each the product of years of costly design work and it was clear that developing any of them into a final finished product was never going to be cheap. It was, however, estimated that by 1995 there would be more than 500 SSTs in service around the world and it was supposed that a substantial investment in the technology would see a substantial return.

The three competing designs were submitted to the FAA for review on January 15, 1964, and the NAC-60 was quickly dismissed. Its more rounded nose meant that it would be slower than the other two at Mach 2.65 and there were concerns about the level of noise that it would produce. Boeing and Lockheed were then asked to ensure that their proposals met a more detailed set of requirements. As a result of these requirements, Boeing substantially altered its proposal to become Model 733-790. The tail was larger and longer, the engines were tucked beneath the rear of the fuselage rather than the centre and the body was lengthened significantly. More alterations saw the 733-790 become the 2707-100. Now the swing-wings, when fully swung back, merged into a widened body to form a complete delta shape. There would have been two aisles inside with seats for 300 passengers arrange from the left side of the aircraft to the right in a 2-3-2 formation. Overhead television sets would have been installed at six row intervals in the main cabin but first class passengers would only have to share one between two.

A final deadline of September 1966 for both designs and full-scale mock-ups was set and three months later it was announced that the Boeing bid had been successful. A projected schedule involved prototype construction beginning in 1967 and the setting up of production lines for the production version in 1969. The prototypes would be flight tested in 1970 and the production version would fly in 1972 before entering service in 1974.

The Soviet Tu-144 Charger was superficially similar to Concorde but its hurried construction meant it was unreliable at best. At worst it was downright dangerous.

As work began in earnest, it started to become apparent that the 733-790 was just too heavy. By 1968 the swing-wing mechanism had to be abandoned completely and the gargantuan aircraft had been cut back to a fixed wing type called Model 2707-300. This, though still dwarfing Concorde, had 234 seats and fixed wings. Its fuselage was lengthened too to improve streamlining. It was 1969 before construction of the first prototype could begin – two years later than planned.

As the years dragged by, a growing number of people began to voice concerns about the sonic booms produced by supersonic aircraft. Tests over Oklahoma City in 1965, known as Operation Bongo II, had resulted in numerous complaints about cracked windows, broken plaster and terrified pets. The aviation industry attempted to downplay or even ignore these concerns but the protesters' views filled an ever-growing number of column inches in the American national press and the weight of public opinion began to turn against supersonic aircraft in general and SSTs in particular.

The end was in sight in 1971 when, despite personal support from President Richard Nixon, the project's government funding was cut off. Concorde was already flying and it was evident that the SST race had been lost as Boeing's designers and engineers continued to wrestle with a host of problems thrown up by their enormously complicated aircraft. There were still 115 orders from 25 airlines on the table for the 2707-300, even six each from BOAC (the forerunner of British Airways) and Air France, but nevertheless the US government voted to cancel it. In the months that followed, Boeing had to shed more than 60,000 jobs at its works in Seattle.

THE DARK HORSE

Another nail in the coffin of America's SST hopes came from an entirely unexpected direction. The Russians, having watched the early efforts of Britain and France to create an SST, had secretly set about building their own contender – the Tupolev Tu-144, later codenamed Charger by the West.

Work began in 1963, not long after the British and French teams had pooled their resources and their efforts to create Concorde. In common with other Soviet designs of the period it bore a strong superficial resemblance to the aircraft that inspired it, having four engines fitted beneath its wings in two pods, a drooping nose and a delta wing.

There were rumours of espionage and concerns that there had been a breach of security within either of the two European construction companies but the truth was

RIGHT: Years after its withdrawal from service, NASA used this modified Tu-144 as a flying laboratory to test the effects of supersonic speed.

that if there was a spy, they didn't do their job very well since the Tu-144 proved to be a pale imitation. It needed two retractable canards on its nose to improve lift at low speed and since the Russians didn't have access to turbojet engines, the Tu-144 had to make do with highly inefficient turbofans. If the Tu-144 needed to hit Mach 2 it could only do so by engaging its afterburner – Concorde could cruise at twice the speed of sound without using one. Fuel consumption was incredible and the Charger's range was only half that of Concorde as a result.

The powerful air conditioning system required by the Tu-144 combined with the sound of its engines made travelling on board a deafening experience. Passengers sitting next to one another struggled to make themselves heard and the problem was particularly accute towards the rear of the aircraft where the sound generated was described as 'intolerable' by some. The on board electrical systems were also notoriously unreliable and few flights took place without numerous failures, most of which could be ignored.

The worst problem of all was with the Tu-144's alloy construction. Tests shortly before its introduction showed that inconsistencies in the metals used were likely to result in a higher than usual number of cracks appearing in the airframe. These could quickly spread to result in a

catastrophic failure and the loss of the aircraft. This knowledge kept under wraps at the time and few were aware of just how dangerous the Tu-144 could be.

Despite its shortcomings however, the Tu-144 was at least in the air and was on the point of being able to enter production. To the Americans in 1971 it seemed that they were now in third place. Doubts about the Tu-144 were first raised internationally when the first production version crashed spectacularly at the Paris Air Show in 1973. It entered a dive from which it was unable to recover and went down, killing all six people on board, demolishing 15 houses and killing a further eight on the ground.

Further development work continued and Tupolev remained concerned about the Tu-144's future but by 1975 the Soviet government decided that it could no longer put off its introduction and it began by carrying freight and mail on internal flights. A passenger service began in 1977 but was cancelled after just 55 flights having carried a total of 3194 passengers. An upgraded version, the Tu-144D, was introduced in 1979 purely for freight flights. On July 1, 1983, the Tu-144 was withdrawn from regular services and used thereafter only as a flying laboratory by the Russians and later the American space agency NASA. This left Concorde as the only supersonic transport aircraft in service anywhere in the world.

This Rockwell B-1 Lancer clearly shows the wing and engine layout of the earliest Boeing SST designs, such as the 733-197. USAF Museum

At this early stage, 1967, some entertained hopes that Concorde would fly the following year. These hopes would be cruelly dashed as the prototype's first flight would not be until April 9, 1969.

OPPOSITE: A Bristol Siddeley Olympus 593 jet engine – the heart of Concorde and responsible for its supersonic prowess.

CHAPTER THREE

On the shop floor

Constructing a supersonic airliner

Supersonic aircraft had been built before Concorde but these were highly specialised military machines with, at most, five crew members on board. Concorde had to be built not only to hit Mach 2 but also to keep more than 100 passengers cosseted in the lap of luxury while doing so. Would the British and French 'entente Concordiale' survive the complex construction phase?

The team selected for the difficult task of building Concorde was huge and included scientists, technicians, engineers, designers, aerodynamicists and aero specialists from more than 800 different companies located across Britain and France.

At the beginning of the project in 1962, a treaty was signed by both the British and French sides agreeing to divide the work of building Concorde evenly between both nations. This proved to be much harder to put into practice than it had initially seemed.

A committee was set up to dish out the contracts, with tenders being received from pre-selected subcontractors. These were put in order of preference and the top three then handed over to another committee for evaluation and a final decision.

This decision was made by civil servants who had to keep one eye on the 50/50 split agreement. The result was subcontractors being chosen for political rather than practical reasons, sometimes against the wishes of the design team.

For example, a firm called British Pilkington had just bought the licence for a new type of glass that would've been perfect for Concorde's windows but the Concorde Directing Committee handed the contract over to a French company. They then had to

go about negotiating their own licence to use exactly the same sort of glass.

Boulton Paul and Dassault, British and French aerospace specialists, both tendered for the power supply control systems but Boulton Paul's bid was much cheaper. As a result it won favour with the British contingent on the committee. Dassault though had a lot of pull with the French government and as a result the French committee members were forced to side with the firm's much more expensive bid with the excuse that Dassault was more experienced in producing power supply control systems. Twelve months of arguing ensued before common sense prevailed and the Boulton Paul bid was selected.

When the fully assembled control systems were ready, Boulton Paul had them sent over to France so that the French Concorde assembly team could install them on the aircraft. The French, though, insisted on taking the controls to pieces to check them over. They then realised that they didn't know how to put them back together again. The bits were duly boxed up and sent back to Boulton Paul for reassembly while the French prototype aircraft, Concorde 001, waited on the ground. Organisational difficulties aside, the brightest minds in Britain were brought together for a single purpose – whether it

was Hawker-Siddeley working on the air conditioning system, Palmer manufacturing the fuel filters or Dunlop making the wheels and brakes.

French firms too went all out to make the project become a reality. Among them were Auxilec, which made Concorde's alternators, Jaeger which put together the engine monitoring system and Teleflex-Syneravia which manufactured the aircraft's landing lamps.

The focus on Concorde was total with all of the hundreds of firms involved being jointly coordinated by the British Aircraft Corporation (BAC) and Aerospatiale.

It wasn't just the number of companies involved that made the task of building Concorde so complex either. Whole production processes had to be invented and new precision tools capable of cutting intricate parts from solid aluminium had to be made. Concorde had to be made without using any welded joints, since these would be vulnerable to the severe stresses of flying at supersonic speeds, and this in itself required new ways of working using electron beams.

The distance between the British and French main production centres at Bristol and Toulouse proved to be a headache. They were more than 570 miles apart as the crow flies – or more than 820 miles if items

such as blueprints had to be sent by road. The other firms involved were also widely spread across both countries. Teams of engineers had to be set up just to coordinate the vast process, chase up orders and ensure everything got where it needed to go in good time.

The production of each Concorde followed the same pattern. The first stage of construction was to put together the central fuselage, with wings pre-attached, from the six sections manufactured at Aerospatiale's facilities in Marignane and Toulouse in Southern France and Bouguenais in Western France. To these were added the nose and tail sections that had been built by BAC's Weybridge factory. The French sections needed for the British production line were flown over using a pair of huge Aero Spacelines Super Guppy transport aircraft and the British sections were flown to France in return.

Putting the carefully made aluminium segments together required overhead cranes that ran on rails fitted to the ceiling of the production facilities. As this was being done, the fuel tanks built into the wings had to be sealed using a chemical called Viton which had been developed to withstand the extremes of temperature associated with high altitude and supersonic flight. During each flight, it was expected that Concorde's fuel itself would heat up to over 75C. Lining up the wing sections and locking them together also involved fitting together the wiring for the aircraft's delicate electrical flight control systems – a highly intricate task.

Once the wings were complete, their leading edges and tips were fitted separately. The internal fuselage wiring was now added. This required thousands of wires to be threaded through the central portion of Concorde. They had been pre-assembled into a harness which had to be carried over and then lowered into the airframe. Next came the elevons, the rudder and the visor attachment for the aircraft's slender nose section – though not the protective visor itself.

Fitting the undercarriage, still kept within its plastic wrapping at this stage to protect its sensitive hydraulics from the ingress of dirt and grease, was far from simple and involving lifting the entire aircraft up off the ground on jacks. The four Olympus 593 engines were now fitted. These were constructed in large part by Bristol Siddeley Engines, which became part of Rolls-Royce in 1966. While the part of the engine that actually produced the power was 100% British, the jet pipe, nozzles and reheat were built by the French SNECMA organisation.

The engines were brought up to the aircraft but before they could be fitted into position the air intakes and the engine bays themselves, made at Filton, had to undergo a series of final checks. They were manufactured from alloys, titanium and stainless steel to ensure that they were up to the job of containing the immense heat generated by the engines when they were running at maximum power.

With the 593s in position, the nose visor was fitted and checks were carried out on all the door and window seals to ensure that they were waterproof. The aircraft was then towed to the factory paint shop where it received a coat of white 'high reflectivity' paint. This was designed to help reflect and radiate out the heat generated by the aircraft during supersonic flight. It had a reflectivity rating of 80 out of 100 compared to the rating for normal white gloss paint which varies between about 45 and 50 out of 100. Even then, during its service lifetime

ABOVE: Concorde surrounded by its many technicians and draftsmen in Bristol on November 30, 1967.

each Concorde aircraft had to be repainted every three years due to the high level of stress suffered by the paint. Airline insignia were then sprayed on in a similar formula of durable paint.

The final phase of construction was to add the multitude of instruments needed on the flight deck, the radio and navigation equipment and the interior fixtures and fittings such as carpets, seats, luggage racks, panelling, galley areas, toilets and safety features such as slides and lift rafts. All of this was done with the aircraft sitting on the tarmac outside the hangar so that the workers inside had the maximum amount of space to operate.

While the basic process of building Concorde remained the same throughout the construction of the 20 airframes eventually completed, there were significant differences between the early prototypes and the later pre-production and then production versions as the results of ongoing tests came through and were analysed. Changes ranged from very minor tweaks to complete revisions of major aspects of the aircraft.

The areas that saw the most significant alterations between the prototypes and the

Bags of space?

Every square inch of space on board Concorde had to earn its keep and baggage was a key consideration during construction. It was considered that a luxury aircraft should offer an adequate amount of space for passengers' belongings but the demands of supersonic travel meant that in practice baggage had to be squeezed into two separate compartments.

The hand luggage allowance for Concorde was a medium sized bag plus a laptop computer or briefcase. For the hold, you could bring with you baggage weighing no more than 26lb (12kg) – less than two average density bowling balls – and measuring no more than 22 x 16 x 8in (55 x 40 x 20cm), the size of a smallish suitcase.

The lower of Concorde's two baggage compartments could hold about 227cu ft or 6.4cu m while the upper was larger at 476cu ft or 13.48cu m but even together they could only hold a volume of luggage equivalent to the space in the back of 16 Ford Focus hatchbacks with the rear seats folded down.

Each baggage compartment was fitted with its own internal lighting and smoke detection system and heated or cooled with air from the flight compartment.

The British pre-production Concorde 01, G-AXDN on December 13, 1971, at Filton. This was the first version of the aircraft to feature a fully glazed visor.

final production version were the nose and visor, the wings and the rear portion of the fuselage. The engines too underwent significant refinements. For the first two Concorde airframes, 001 and 002, the visor, the upper section of the nose that could be raised for maximum aerodynamic efficiency or lowered for better visibility, was made from an aluminium alloy.

Within this large protective plates there were small cut-out sections through which the pilots could see where they were going, albeit very narrowly. This was never intended as a permanent feature but it was brought about through necessity since development work on the glass required for the fully glazed visor had yet to be completed. It was ready for the pre-production types, 101 and 102, however. Once fitted it allowed extremely good forward visibility.

Concorde's wings appear at a distance to have a simple and straightforward curve. But for anyone viewing them at close quarters this impression swiftly vanishes. The leading edge is a complex and finely honed combination of drooping and twisting form. This is the result of an exhaustive programme of wind tunnel testing and fine detail alterations, particularly to the tips, the outer camber and the leading edge itself were continually being made throughout development to ensure Concorde handled well at high speeds. The end of Concorde's tail was lengthened during the development process and reshaped. The production version of Concorde differs markedly from the prototypes in having the upper line of its fuselage running much further beyond the rear tail fin and remaining almost horizontal while the lower portion swoops up to meet it at the end. This refinement not only reduced drag at supersonic speed, it also gave the aircraft much needed additional fuel capacity.

The process of deciding what materials should be used in the construction was a painstaking one. The initial choice of an aluminium alloy as the main structural material was made because Concorde would not have to fly at speeds much greater than Mach 2. Aluminium could comfortably handle the stresses involved in reaching this speed but could not tolerate speeds much beyond Mach 2.5. Even with this decision made however, the engineers selecting the alloy had to work their way through thousands of different specimens before they were satisfied that they had the right combination of metals. Tests were carried out for resistance to fatigue and corrosion as well as basic strength and mechanical properties.

Another test was for something aero engine designers knew as 'creep'. This is the gradual warping of metals that takes place when loaded structures are repeatedly exposed to extreme temperatures, particularly heat. While jet engine designers regularly had to factor in creep this was something new to airframe engineers for whom it had never previously been an issue. Checking for creep resistance involved

Down the hatch

One of the most essential components of any passenger airliner is its toilets but Concorde presented a particular problem for its legion of designers and engineers in this regard. How do you eject waste water at high altitude without it instantly freezing up, even before it has left the aircraft?

With a total of three passenger toilets on board, it was a problem that had to be solved. The answer was to install individual heating systems into the toilet drains. These consisted of a heating element and thermostat attached to each pipe. Whenever a thermostat detected a temperature drop to below 4.4°C in the lowest section of pipe, it would activate the element and heat the pipe to 12.8°C.

This ensured that waste leaving the aircraft would at least be able to clear the fuselage before icing up completely and beginning its long fall to the ground or ocean below.

The interior of Britain's first Concorde begins to take shape.

Roll out the (blue) carpet

During supersonic flight the entire fuselage of Concorde stretched by up to 20cm and the engineers building the aircraft had to create every fixture and fitting with this in mind. As a result, Concorde's flame-resistant carpet had to be pre-stretched and secured at points all the way along the length of the aircraft.

The carpet also had to include five 'flaps' – points where crews could lift it up to access important gubbins beneath such as the emergency nose undercarriage release lever,

the main landing gear release and undercarriage observation access.

Whenever the carpet needed a thorough cleaning it had to be completely removed from the aircraft before being shampooed, dried, re-fireproofed with a Borax and Boric acid dip and re-treated with chemicals to restore its anti-static properties.

Concorde's galley and other vestibule areas were covered with fire-resistant PVC flooring.

subjecting samples to round the clock variations in temperature using automatically controlled testing installations designed and built just for that purpose.

Eventually, the alloy chosen was a mix of copper and aluminium known to the British team as RR58 and to the French as AU2GN – even though it was the same thing on both sides of the Channel. Its manufacturer, High Duty Alloys Ltd, called it Hiduminium from Hi(gh) du(ty) (alu)minium. It had originally been designed for use in the manufacture of gas turbine blades but High Duty Alloys assured the Concorde team that it could be made into components of whatever shape or size they wanted. Concorde's other materials also had to undergo rigorous

testing to make absolutely certain they were suitable for an aircraft that would be placed under such enormous strain during its regular passenger carrying duties. These included a substantial quantity of titanium and stainless steel plus a range of plastics, paints, adhesives, sealants and other non-ferrous materials.

The Olympus 593B engines fitted to the prototype Concordes were found to produce too much smoke during takeoff and landing so the two developers, Rolls-Royce and SNECMA decided to fit the aircraft with a new combustion chamber. This was an 'annular' type which, when used together with a vaporising fuel injector system, gave Concorde a virtually smoke-free exhaust.

The engine designers also had to find a way of coping with different temperatures of air encountered by different parts of the Olympus. Flying at Mach 2, the air entering the engine was about –60°C but it was about 130°C by the time it reached the face of the engine and 550°C when it left the high-pressure compressor.

Later versions of Concorde therefore had titanium and nickel alloy parts. These could not only withstand variations in temperature – they could also stand up better against foreign objects such as birds or debris which might be ingested.

Building Concorde was one thing but actually getting it into airline service was quite another.

In the air
Prototype rollouts and first flights

F-WTSS

It took a massive effort to make the first two prototypes of Concorde, 001 in France and 002 in Britain, and these aircraft were still a long way from the final finished product. But when the first one took to the skies on live TV the world sat up and took notice.

MAIN IMAGE: The rolling out ceremony of the prototype 001 supersonic airliner concorde at Toulouse in France on December 11, 1967.

LEFT: Another view of 001 during its rollout in Toulouse.

CHAPTER FOUR

France's Concorde 001 makes its first public appearance. At this stage it was anticipated that the aircraft's maiden flight would take place on February 28, 1968 – more than a year before it actually first flew.

Air traffic between Filton in Bristol and Toulouse became increasingly busy in 1967 as the Concorde project neared its first major goal – completion of the prototypes.

Every component and the systems they comprised, whether they were built in Britain or France, were checked and double-checked as the two aircraft took shape in their respective hangars.

The nose mechanism of Concorde received particular attention since it was essential that this part of the aircraft operated correctly every time. There were four Olympus 593 engines and if one failed there were procedures that could be followed to bring the aircraft back down safely. A failure of the nose could result in serious problems during takeoff or landing.

As with the Fairey Delta before it, Concorde was designed with a sharply pointed nose for aerodynamic efficiency at high speeds. Wind tunnel tests showed that this shape greatly reduced drag but it was also clear that having only a small slit to see out over a very long nose made it difficult for the aircraft's pilot to see where he was going.

This problem was particularly acute in Concorde's case since the aircraft, with its delta wing, would need to point its nose high up in the air to generate sufficient lift for takeoff and during landings. The answer was to find a way of allowing the pointed nose to 'droop' away from the pilot's windscreen, giving a much broader and clearer field of vision when it was needed most. During

flight, when only forward visibility was required, a visor built into the droop nose covered the windscreen. This tinted and heat-resistant shield maintained the aircraft's aerodynamic shape and was easily retracted into the nose when it drooped.

The pilot could control the nose and visor from the cockpit with a four position lever linked to the mechanism via a hydraulic system. A series of lights indicated the nose's current position. The first position was fully up with visor in place, the second was fully up with visor down – either for subsonic flight or window cleaning, the third was a 5° droop with visor down for taxiing and takeoff and the fourth was visor down with the nose drooped by 12.5° for landing.

In the event of the main system failing, there was a backup hydraulic system and control to unlock the nose which would then droop under its own weight or the pressure of the air flowing around it. If even this failed, there was a third and final option – a manual release which would allow the nose to fall by 5°. This would give the pilot just enough of a view to effect a landing.

Concorde's prototype's featured a metal visor with just two glass panels for the pilot and co-pilot to see out of. In the production version, as had always been intended, there were six transparent panels. Each was made from three separate sheets of glass, two thick outer sheets and a thin interlayer. In all it was 1.5in thick and was impact resistant in addition to its other properties.

Both the visor and windscreen were subjected to bird impact tests while the cabin

windows along both sides of the aircraft were stressed with one deliberately pre-failed to see how the structure would cope with the loss of a window at high altitude.

Beyond the nose mechanism, all of Concorde's electronic, hydraulic and mechanical systems were tested in a wide range of temperatures to ensure that they were up to the task of operating at supersonic speeds. A number of full scale ground test rigs were developed for this purpose.

One at Toulouse was used to test the flight controls and the electrical and hydraulic systems they operated including the undercarriage. Attached to the systems rig was Concorde's first flight simulator. Though primitive by modern standards, this simulated flight deck allowed 001's first test pilot André Turcat to familiarise himself with the controls and their operation before he ever climbed aboard the actual aircraft. The main function of the simulator though was to fine tune the design of the controls and systems and their responses to particular situations. It was even used in conjunction with the air traffic controllers at Paris's Orly airport to see how Concorde could be integrated into their existing operations.

The British had a less complex flight simulator for pilot and air crew familiarisation but this was primarily used to test Concorde's systems. Another rig in Britain was used to test the fuel tanks and their associated components. A large movable platform was fitted with an accurate recreation of the aircraft's 11 main

The last resort – escaping Concorde

While it was hoped that the early test flights of Concorde would go off without a hitch this was by no means guaranteed.

In the event of a catastrophic failure there were no ejection seats for the crew and observers but there were parachutes. Still, getting out of such a large fast jet alive was a task fraught with danger.

The only way out with even a chance of success was an escape hatch built into the floor of all prototype and pre-production Concordes. This was held closed by explosive bolts which could be blown in an emergency.

Flight crew and observers were usually wearing pressure suits and helmets but even with these the chances of walking away from an out of control Concorde would have been extremely slim.

Even during level flight at relatively low altitude getting out would have been problematic. Blowing the hatch at 60,000ft would have caused the cabin to depressurise and the aircraft to climb dramatically. At this altitude there was very little chance of survival no matter what sort of gear you were wearing.

If you had to jump out of this hatch in a prototype Concorde you were in serious trouble. Editor

The first formal taxiing trial of 001 on August 21, 1968. The trial was carried out to test the hydraulic and braking systems.

and two reserve tanks and this was then pressurised, heated and cooled to simulate different altitudes, speeds and situations. Designers and engineers could then make detailed modifications as they were required without having to remove bodywork panels.

A pair of rigs were constructed for electrical systems tests, one each for the generation and distribution systems. Rigs were also developed for the engine's air intakes and for every aspect of the undercarriage from wheels to tyres and brakes.

Once everything was in place and the first prototype, 001, was completed it was rolled out of its assembly hall in Toulouse on December 11, 1967, for a public reception. This was the first time anyone outside the Concorde programme had seen the finished article and reports were quickly flashed around the world via TV, radio, newspapers and magazines. British and French taxpayers could finally see where all their money had been

spent following years of design and construction work.

The first flight of 001 took place on Sunday, March 2, 1969, having been postponed from the day before due to foggy conditions. Toulouse welcomed invited guests from all over the world for the occasion including representatives of airlines, politicians and hundreds of journalists including TV news cameramen and reporters preparing for live broadcasts. The weather still seemed poor but a Mirage jet fighter was sent up and reported that conditions were indeed suitable.

A public address system installed for the occasion announced to the crowds that Concorde's crew – chief test pilot Turcat, co-pilot Jacques Guignard, flight engineer Michel Rétif, chief flight test observer Henri Perrier, assistant chief of flight test observer Jean Belon and flight observer Claude Durand – were on board and undertaking pre-flight checks. The aircraft's engines were powered up, emergency vehicles moved into position and bird scarer

vehicles went about ensuring that the runway was clear. It was about 3.30pm.

The aircraft taxiied into position at the end of the runway to await final clearance from the control tower and when it was given Concorde's brakes were released and it began to move, slowly to begin with but then rapidly gathering pace until the nose wheel lifted off the ground. It was now 3.40pm.

At this point those watching at home in Britain heard the commentator, Raymond Baxter, enthusiastically announcing: "Nose comes up to 20°, she's airborne, she flies, Concorde flies." The aircraft climbed rapidly after takeoff with the same Mirage fighter flying chase and soared high into the sky before disappearing from view. Just 27 minutes later, after reaching 10,000ft and speeds no greater than 300mph, Turcat brought 001 back down for a faultless landing with the aid of a tail parachute and reverse thrust. The crew emerged at the top of the steps, led by Turcat who gave a thumbs-up signal with both hands. Returning to the airport, the captain could not stop himself grinning and said: "Finally the big bird flies, and I can say now that it flies pretty well."

Among the observers was Brian Trubshaw whose own moment of glory was soon to come as the first British pilot of Concorde.

LEFT: Concorde 001 taxiies briefly under its own power for the first time at Toulouse on August 19, 1968.

BELOW: With French test pilot André Turcat at the controls, 001 takes off for the first time at Toulouse-Blagnac airport on March 2, 1969. It flew for 27 minutes.

ABOVE: Brian Trubshaw is at the controls as Concorde 002 comes in to land at Fairford Airfield, Gloucestershire, after its inaugural flight.

RIGHT: Concorde 002, the British prototype, gets airborne for the first time at Filton airport in Bristol on April 9, 1969. The maiden flight lasted just 22 minutes.

BELOW: A Gloster Meteor surveillance plane, upper right, is dwarfed by Concorde 001 on March 8, 1969, during its second flight. Concorde's undercarriage was pulled up for the first time during the flight which lasted 61 minutes.

"I was terribly impressed by the way the whole flight was conducted," he said to reporters. "It was most professional and I would like to congratulate André on the way he handled this performance."

More but less publicised test flights took place from Toulouse during that same month and on April 9 Britain's first Concorde, 002, was readied for its own maiden flight. Trubshaw gathered his team together and boarded the aircraft. The team consisted of co-pilot John Cochrane; senior flight test engineer John Allan; flight engineer Brian Watts and Mike Addley and Peter Holding, both flight test observers.

The pre-flight preparations on board took more than an hour before permission was granted to start the engines. Cochrane communicated with air traffic control and was given clearance to taxi and Trubshaw started the operation. The first two attempts had to be aborted due to an airspeed indicator problem but it was all systems go for the third attempt.

Taxiing had been practised a number of times before but this time it was the real thing and once again a crowd of observers looked on as Concorde left the ground. In flight, Trubshaw went through a pre-scheduled sequence of tests before heading for Fairford airfield. There was a slight hiccup with the two radio altimeters but this problem was swiftly overcome.

Concorde 002 touched down at Fairford and slowed to a stop with reverse thrust and brake parachute deployed after 22 minutes of flight time. Fairford had been designated as the first flight base of Concorde because of its 9993ft long runway. There was a VIP reception party before a debriefing and the crew's return to Filton where another reception had been organised.

At Filton, Trubshaw and his crew were handed a Concorde 002 cake especially made for the occasion by pioneering aviatrix Sheila Scott, who two years later became the first person to fly over the North Pole in a light aircraft. The second test flight of Concorde 002 was postponed because Brian Trubshaw had an accident with a saw and

hurt his hand and he was the only one cleared to captain the aircraft. He was soon declared fit again and the test flights were resumed. Turcat came to Britain and worked alongside Trubshaw in piloting Concorde 002 and the pooled resources and intelligence of Britain and France continued to be put into the single-minded operation on both sides of the Channel.

Neither of the two prototypes had been pushed too hard on their first time out and now, with the data gathered from their respective flights, a further battery of tests ensued to ensure that they would be up to the challenge of more strenuous flying manoeuvres and ultimately flying at twice the speed of sound.

The ticking clock – Concorde on a time limit

The celebrations and bonhomie that accompanied the first flights of Concorde served to mask the fact that the aircraft's financial backers, the British and French governments, were desperate for quick results.

Both development teams were under pressure to get their aircraft not just airborne but supersonic, if only to prove that the sums had been done correctly and that Concorde could indeed achieve sustainable high speed flight.

Everyone wanted to know whether Concorde would be able to do all that was expected of it because every minute and every hour of the project saw further large sums of cash being expended. The test flights themselves were tremendously expensive due to the amount of fuel being consumed by the aircraft.

It was therefore something of a relief when Concorde demonstrated that it could take off and land without any problems. Test pilots reported that its handling was better than had been predicted and equipment such as TV cameras to monitor the rear landing gear was found to be superfluous.

After the first flights in March and April 1969, as each day passed, there was still the question of whether supersonic flight could be attained. It was a question that would not be cleared up until that October.

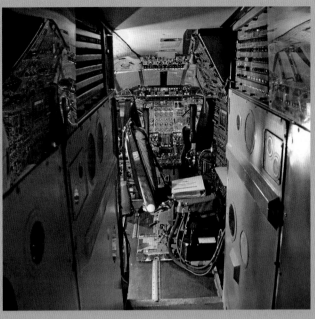

The interior of a development version of Concorde. There are few seats beyond the cockpit – just banks of instruments. Editor

Concorde 002 captain Brian Trubshaw (left) and co-pilot John Cochrane (right) hold a cake presented to them by veteran aviator Sheila Scott at Filton, after their aircraft's maiden flight.

Up, up and away

Supersonic trials and airline customers

The initial rush of enthusiasm for Concorde had seen airlines queuing up to place their orders and by 1969 the sense of anticipation was palpable. As the year drew to a close, both prototypes took their first supersonic flights and it seemed as though nothing could put a dampener on its success...

Concorde had proven that it could fly in early 1969 but there was still work to do before the two prototypes could be brought up to speed for their first supersonic flight. Sixteen airlines had by now each ordered their own small Concorde fleet – totalling 76 aircraft. It was estimated that around 150 would need to be sold if the British and French governments which had bankrolled the project were to break even but this was still a promising start.

Shortly after 001's successful first flight the governments authorised production of seven more Concorde airframes – two pre-production examples, two ground test frames and the first three production aircraft, known as 201, 202 and 203.

The appearance of both 001 and 002 flying together at the Paris Air Show in June 1969 saw enthusiasm for the aircraft soar and huge crowds both on the airfield and in Paris itself watched as the graceful white aircraft were put through their paces.

Structural testing was begun on the first ground test frame in France in September 1969. The frame was progressively placed under pressure at room temperature using 80 hydraulic jacks controlled by servo-motors to see how it would respond. When these tests were successfully concluded they were repeated at temperatures ranging from 120ºC to -10ºC using an array of 35,000 infrared lamps for heat and 70,000l of liquid nitrogen for cooling.

This work took three years to complete and resulted in Concorde being certified as capable of bearing a takeoff weight of 385,000lb. Early on however, it was clear that the aircraft would be able to withstand the rigors of supersonic flight with relative ease and plans were set for the first supersonic test.

During its 45th test flight, on October 1, 1969, Concorde 001 went faster than the speed of sound for the first time at an altitude of 36,000ft. It hit Mach 1.5, 1125 mph, for nine minutes. With the onus on maintaining customer interest, four airline pilots, one each from BOAC, Air France, Pan American and TWA, were invited to take 001 for a supersonic flight. Each received two sessions in the Concorde simulator at Toulouse before flying the aircraft up to Mach 1.2. As had been hoped, they issued a favourable report at the end of their experience. On November 12 Concorde successfully made its first landing at night and in December the British and French governments gave approval for the next batch of three production aircraft to be constructed – 204, 205 and 206.

002 went supersonic for the first time on March 25, 1970, hitting Mach 1.15, and two months later it was being used to test a new engine nozzle type which was intended to improve the aerodynamics of the production model Concorde, reduce its weight and make it quieter too. A flight to Heathrow in September resulted in a number of complaints from people living nearby – an ominous sign of things to come. Both prototypes reached Mach 2 in November.

Two months later the total number of supersonic flights successfully carried out by the two prototypes had reached 100. On January 20, the total estimated cost of developing Concorde, £825 million, was discussed in the House of Commons, as was a looming uncertainty over the future of sales to the US. The environmental lobby was gaining the upper hand in America and the writing was on the wall for the Boeing 2707 supersonic transport programme which was cancelled in March.

CHAPTER FIVE

OPPOSITE: A view of Concorde 002, registered as G-BSST, during trials in 1970.

THIS PAGE: Britain's pre-production, Concorde 101, G-AXDN, during its Filton roll-out.

ABOVE: Concorde 002 sets off on its first supersonic flight with chief test pilot Brian Trubshaw at the controls.

RIGHT: Concorde 001, right, and Concorde 002 are pictured together in Toulouse, France, on May 7, 1971.

During the discussion, MP Patrick Wall asked Conservative Minister of Aviation Supply Frederick Corfield: "Could my right honourable friend say anything about operating Concorde over the United States, and whether we are likely to be given clearance for that?"

Corfield replied: "There is the problem of the noise restrictions which are the subject of discussion in the United States, and I am keeping in close touch with how they are going. They could affect the issue very much indeed." In fact, the Concorde test programme had just suffered a setback. During a supersonic test run, part of 001's engine air intake system had broken off and been sucked into the engine itself, resulting in damage and forcing the pilot to shut it down. The aircraft flew back to Toulouse for repairs and a redesign.

Back in the House of Commons, Labour MP Willie Hamilton asked Corfield whether he would establish a ceiling on the Concorde project above which the public purse would no longer pick up the bill. Corfield's answer was a brusque: "No."

Undeterred, Hamilton countered with: "Does the right honourable gentleman recognise that an increasing volume of public opinion fears that this might be the most expensive white elephant in British aviation history?"

As he had throughout the discussion, Corfield fell back on the cross party

consensus that had developed on Concorde, primarily thanks to Labour MP Tony Benn who was an ardent supporter of Concorde – which was being built in his constituency. He said: "I cannot think of any more unwise course than to fix a purely arbitrary ceiling at this stage. As I have said on a number of occasions – I have always taken this view, as has the right honourable member for Bristol, South-East (Benn) – this stage would be the least sensible stage at which to consider cancelling Concorde."

In April, the British and French governments gave the go ahead for the construction of yet another four production aircraft, 207, 208, 209 and 210.

May saw 001 fly to Dakar and back, the longest trip so far undertaken by Concorde before it was then sent on a two week tour of South America in August. A third

Concorde, the first of the two pre-production aircraft and known as G-AXDN or Concorde 101, was rolled out at Filton on September 20. Its first flight was on December 17. Three days before that, the American Federal Aviation Agency announced that Concorde was within American airport noise limits.

This was good news. What was not such good news was the selling pricing formula for Concorde customers which was announced by Corfield in the House of Commons on December 22 – £13 million was the starting point but there was "no single price for the aircraft. The price paid by an individual airline will depend on the exact terms of the contract negotiated in each case". As it turned out, £13 million was a long way off the eventual asking price for a single Concorde.

Airlines that ordered Concorde

Pan Am
Six aircraft optioned on June 3, 1963, two more optioned on July 24, 1966. Cancelled on January 31, 1973.

Air France
Six aircraft optioned on June 3, 1963. Eventually bought seven aircraft.

BOAC (British Airways from March 31, 1974)
Six aircraft optioned on June 3, 1963. Eventually bought seven aircraft.

Continental
Three aircraft optioned on July 24, 1963. Cancelled in March 1973.

American Airlines
Four aircraft optioned on October 7, 1963, two more optioned on January 16, 1964. Cancelled in February 1973.

Trans World Airlines (TWA)
Four aircraft optioned on October 16, 1963, two more optioned on March 30, 1964. Cancelled in February 1973.

Middle East Airlines – Air Liban (MEA)
Two aircraft optioned on December 4, 1963, two more optioned on January 16, 1964. Cancelled in June 1973.

Qantas
Four aircraft optioned on March 19, 1964. Never formally cancelled.

Air India
Two aircraft optioned on July 15, 1964. Cancelled in February 1975.

Japan Airlines
Three aircraft optioned on September 30, 1965. Cancelled in 1973.

Sabena
Two aircraft optioned on December 1, 1965. Cancelled in February 1973.

Eastern Airlines
Two aircraft optioned on June 28, 1966, two more optioned on August 15, 1966, and another two on April 28, 1967. Cancelled in February 1973.

United Airlines
Six aircraft optioned on June 29, 1966. Cancelled in November 1972.

Braniff
Three aircraft optioned on September 1, 1966. Cancelled in February 1973

Lufthansa
Three aircraft optioned on February 16, 1967. Cancelled in April 1973.

Air Canada
Four aircraft optioned on March 1, 1967. Cancelled in June 1972.

Civil Aviation Administration of China (CAAC)
Two aircraft optioned on July 24, 1972, one more optioned on August 28, 1972. The first two cancelled in December 1979, the third in February 1980.

Iran Air
One aircraft optioned on October 8, 1972. Orders for two confirmed. Cancelled in February 1980.

ABOVE: Models display Hardy Amies uniform designs for cabin crews of British Airways Concorde in London. The unveiling was on January 14, 1976 – just a week before the first commercial BA Concorde service.

> **CONCORDE MADE ITS FIRST APPEARANCE IN GERMANY AT THE HANOVER AIR SHOW ON APRIL 22-23 WITH 002 DOING THE HONOURS.**

The first three Concorde aircraft were gathered together for the first time at RAF Fairford on January 6, 1972, and further testing was carried out. French pre-production aircraft, 102, was completed in February and 101 went supersonic for the first time. A month later, the governments gave the go ahead for another six production models – 211, 212, 213, 214, 215 and 216.

Concorde made its first appearance in Germany at the Hanover Air show on April 22-23 with 002 doing the honours. In June the same aircraft began a sales tour in the Far East and Australia.

The first cancelled order came in June 1972. Back in 1967, Air Canada had said it wanted four aircraft. Now they were surplus to requirements. Five months later, United Airlines also backed out. It had wanted six aircraft but now said that Concorde did not meet its needs because its flights were mainly across the continental US, where the sonic booms it generated were likely to result in both complaints and lawsuits. Whether these were likely to be successful or not, United didn't want to have to contest them.

It was a retreat from Concorde that was to become a rout. While the environmental lobby had certainly had an impact, as long as Pan American World Airways remained interested in Concorde, many other world airlines felt they had to retain their purchase orders. Pan Am was America's largest airline and where it led, others followed. But Pan Am was in trouble by the beginning of 1973.

The company had made losses totalling $150 million since 1968 but a new company president, William Seawell, had been brought on board in 1971 to stem the decline. During his first full year in charge he had managed to reduce the firm's losses from a crippling $46 million to a slightly more manageable $29 million. Having looked carefully at the numbers, and with the demise of the Boeing 2707, he began to

Pre-production Concorde 101, left, is seen parked up next to British prototype, 002, at the British Aircraft Corporation's flight test base at Fairford on December 17, 1971. The difference between their visors is clearly visible.

see Concorde as a risk that Pan Am could ill afford to take.

Pan Am's position had been improved in part by the launch of a different Boeing offering – the 747. While it couldn't go supersonic and it didn't provide a high-end luxury service, it could cram in up to 375 passengers per trip compared to Concorde's 100. There was no issue with sonic booms and it was proving to be both highly reliable and cost effective. Seawell's accountants and engineers told him that Concorde was likely to consume two or three times as much fuel per passenger as the Boeing 747. At the beginning of 1973, the fuel crisis that would later shake the world was 10 months away but even at relatively low prices, it still made good sense for an ailing airline to make each drop of fuel count.

To make matters worse, as part of the ongoing effort to shore up Pan Am, Seawell had just been forced to go through the arduous process of renegotiating Pam Am's $270 million credit agreement with its financial backers. Buying Concorde would mean having to go back again, cap in hand, to ask for yet more money.

The figure of £13 million to buy one aircraft that had been confidently announced by Frederick Corfield in Parliament was a little off since Pan Am would have had to pay somewhere in the region of £20 million each for them. A

Boeing 747 cost substantially less.

In 1973 it had been nearly 10 years since the founder of Pan Am, Juan Trippe formally declared his interest in Concorde and now it fell to Seawell to back out of the arrangement, which he did on January 31. Having already got wind of what was about to happen and having been looking for a way out itself, TWA followed suit just minutes later.

The following day a Lufthansa spokesman suggested that Concorde should be substantially redesigned. The firm's order was formally cancelled in April. Sitting on the sidelines while the disaster unfolded, Sir George Edwards, chairman of the British Aircraft Corporation, said: "We should not describe this as a fatal blow, but it's a hell of a setback."

American Airlines followed in the wake of Pan Am and TWA, ditching its order for six aircraft, as did Belgian airline Sabena which had wanted two, Eastern Airlines with its six and US-based Braniff which had wanted three. Continental cancelled its three in March and Middle East Airlines followed in June. This effectively removed any supersonic competition Japan Air Lines might have faced so it too cancelled its order. Beyond BOAC and Air France, this left just three 'foreign' orders on the books. Air India still wanted the two aircraft it had ordered in July 1964, the Civil Aviation Administration of China was keeping its

order for three aircraft made during 1972 and Iran Air maintained its two orders.

Qantas, Australia's largest and oldest airline, had previously believed that Concorde would be ideal for flying business executives from Sydney to London via Singapore and had options on four aircraft. It was, however, becoming increasingly worried about Concorde's range. While BAC and Aérospatiale insisted that the aircraft could easily complete the 3939 mile trek from Sydney to Singapore fully loaded with fuel to spare, Qantas wasn't so sure. It therefore never chose to take up its options, although it never formally cancelled them either.

Shellshocked by the mass cancellation of orders, the Concorde constructors pressed ahead in the hope that if the nationalised carriers BOAC and Air France could make it profitable, the others might come back on board. Then on June 3 a Tu-144 Charger crashed during the Paris Air Show killing 14 people – six on board and another eight on the ground. While the accident had nothing to do with the Tu-144's supersonic capabilities or Concorde, it played into the hands of those who had been suggesting for years that supersonic transport aircraft were simply unsafe.

Fatigue testing was begun on the British test frame in August 1973. It was wrapped in an airtight sleeve with a gap left all the way round. Heated and cooled air was then

circulated around it using five fans powered by 2300hp motors. Yet more hydraulic jacks were used to simulate the effects of both internal and external pressure.

The effects of air conditioning and fuel circulation were also simulated during the experiments. The goal was to reproduce the effects of fatigue on the airframe – the like of which it could expect to encounter in regular airline service – and one hour in the rig was the equivalent of a three hour flight.

A total of 6800 cycles had to be completed before the aircraft could achieve certification.

Concorde made its first visit to America on September 18 when 102 touched down during the grand opening of the Dallas-Fort Worth airport. Less than two months later, on December 6, the first production version of Concorde, 201, finally made its maiden flight from Toulouse. The testing was over and 201 stayed aloft for two hours and 40 minutes, hitting Mach 1.57.

Production continued but limited to 16 aircraft plus the two prototypes and two pre-production versions. There was more bad news in 1975 when Air India cancelled its orders but by now it hardly mattered. Concorde received its French Certificate of Airworthiness on October 9 and its British equivalent on December 5 – clearing the way for the aircraft to begin commercial operations. Concorde had been flying for seven years but it had finally taken off.

ABOVE: Air France's Concorde 205, F-BVFA, prepares to depart from Paris Charles de Gaulle Airport on January 21, 1976, for its first commercial flight. The destination is Rio de Janeiro.

BELOW: Taking off on its maiden commercial flight is British Airways Concorde 206, registered as G-BOAA, bound for Bahrain on January 21, 1976.

Chief Concorde test pilot Brian Trubshaw in the cockpit of 002 on September 4, 1970.

Those magnificent men
Concorde's pioneering pilots

Developing Concorde was a difficult process but the skill and professionalism of two men in particular was essential to its success.

Two men had the privilege of being the first to take Concorde off the ground. Frenchman André Turcat was the first, closely followed by Britain's Brian Trubshaw.

Turcat attended the École Polytechnique – an extremely selective institution of higher education operated by the French Ministry of Defence. During the Second World War, he joined the Free French Air Force and continued to serve as an air force pilot when peace was finally declared.

He had shown a cool head and great skill in a number of emergency situations and quickly earned a reputation as one of France's finest. He was assigned to EPNER,

a test pilot school for French airmen and it was not long before he graduated and was assigned to the testing of one of the world's first ramjet-powered aircraft, the breathtaking Nord 1500 Griffon.

Turcat earned more accolades when he flew the Griffon at Mach 2.19 – a feat which gave him important experience for what was to come next after he joined Sud Aviation and became the chief test pilot on the Concorde programme.

As he explained later: "It is strange but I saw very little of the actual aeroplane because it was always covered with people, ladders and so on as they worked on it in the hangar so it was a big day for me too when it was finally unveiled to the world.

They arranged seating like a theatre and there were many dignitaries from all over the world on that day, December 11, 1967.

"Finally the interior hangar doors were slowly opened like theatre curtains and we all saw it properly for the first time. For me it was like seeing my baby son born. Breathtaking. Later when the crowds had gone I was almost alone with Concorde and felt some butterflies in my stomach. I realised that I was going to soon take this baby into the air and with it tens of millions of hours of work for hundreds of people.

"It was more than a year later that we were ready for the first flight of Concorde. The event was announced for Thursday, February 28, but that was a big anti-climax

Brian Trubshaw, captain of Concorde 002, at Fairford, Gloucester, after its successful maiden flight from Filton.

French Concorde crew in 1969, from left, are chief test pilot André Turcat, test pilot Jean Guignard, flight engineer Henri Perrier and flight engineer Michel Retif.

because we had to postpone due to the weather. Hundreds of people were present including the media and we were all disappointed together. However, the final decision was mine and I had full support of everyone on the team and the executives of Sud Aviation. Finally three days later we decided to take off. We had a false start after all our preparations. An alarm indicated that all was not well when I put the first motor into action. The technicians fixed the problem and everything was fine again.

"Finally there was that wonderful moment when we actually left the ground but we didn't party. That was for later. Right now we had a professional job to do and concentrated totally on what we were doing. There were a couple of small problems so I cut the flight short and we landed again after 29 minutes in the air. It was satisfactory, the problems were not unusual.

"When we landed there was time for emotions and I could not stop myself having a big smile. I waved to my wife who had been watching. The words did not come easily when I was asked to comment and I just said Concorde had flown at last – the big bird was in the air. It did not really come home to me until later when people started to stop me in the street and ask to shake my hand or sign an autograph. I realised then that I was part of an amazing history."

When his aircraft for that first flight, 001, was retired to the French Air Museum at Le Bourget on October 19, 1973, Turcat said: "It was too noisy and too smoky. It didn't have the range required for the North Atlantic crossing. It was cluttered with test instrumentation. And it didn't have the clock with the 24 hour dial, with which one never knows the time but which is required by some airlines. Finally, the ashtrays were full. It had to be sent to the museum, the 001, the grandpa, only four-and-a-half flight

years old. But it had seen a damned lot.

"It was the first to carry 140 tonnes supersonically. It had flown from 110 to 40 knots. It had crossed the South Atlantic in two hours and intersected the 45° south parallel. It had dived, climbed, rolled, yawed and surged more than anyone. Four thousand times, maybe, it had been given modifications.

"It had been a docile tool in the hands of 10 test pilots and 20 airline captains. It had been admired in its strength and its elegance, which its successors have even enhanced. It had carried most important persons. It had spent more than one hour in a total eclipse of the sun and no one can, nor will for a long time, beat this unique record. It had measured nitric acid and the stratosphere and seen, at sunset, the ozone layer shadow on the sky. It had given us the biggest thrills of our careers, and heralded a new transport era for the world. In return, we just loved it."

Brian Trubshaw was watching when Turcat took Concorde on its maiden flight – a feat he would accomplish himself with 002 later that same year. Aged 10, Trubshaw saw the Prince of Wales' aircraft land on that beach near his home in Wales and he was smitten with the idea of flight and flying.

He signed up for the RAF aged 18 in 1942 and was sent to the United States to train as a pilot flying Stearman biplanes. Two years later he joined Bomber Command, flying Stirling and Lancaster bombers before transferring a year later to Transport Command.

With the conclusion of the Second World War, Brian joined the King's Flight and found himself piloting George VI and other members of the royal family. During the 1949-50 period he taught at the Empire Flying School and the RAF College at Cranwell in Lincolnshire.

In 1950 he left the RAF and become a test pilot for Vickers Armstrong. In 1964 he was awarded the OBE and by 1966 he was not only chief test pilot but had become director of test flying. Trubshaw worked on the development of several major aircraft including the Valiant V-bomber, the Vanguard, the VC10 and the BAC One-Eleven. However, his greatest hour was yet to come after the chairman of BAC, George Edwards, selected Brian as test pilot. .

"The day we finally took off was something I shall never, ever forget," he said later. "We took our time in checking everything which must have been a test of patience for those observers but an absolute essential for us. Eventually we were off down the runway with extremely rapid acceleration and finally the wheels left the ground and our Concorde was airborne. There was no euphoria at the time though we all felt exhilarated. We had to focus on the job in hand. I have to say though that taking Concorde 002 into the air for the first time was probably the highlight of my aviation career. It was wizard – a cool, calm and collected operation. Later when we went supersonic, it was like being at the controls of a rifle bullet, just amazing."

A few months later he flew 002 over Buckingham Palace on the Queen's official birthday on June 14, 1969. In 1972, he piloted the aircraft on its world tour and remained close to Concorde throughout the rest of his career in which he became divisional director and general manager of the Filton works of British Aerospace from 1980 to 1986. In 1999 he was a passenger as Concorde retraced his first flight to mark its 30th birthday. When Trubshaw died peacefully in his sleep in March 2001, tributes poured in for the man who said in his autobiography: "It is not unreasonable to look upon Concorde as a miracle."

She left school aged 15 but Barbara Harmer later got her A-levels, paid for her own flying lessons and ended up piloting Concorde.

And a magnificent lady too...

Concorde pilot Barbara Harmer

Only three women ever flew Concorde and two of them were French. The only female Brit ever to take the controls had originally trained as a hairdresser...

As the youngest of four sisters and having left school aged 15 to pursue a career as a hairdresser, few would have believed that 24 years later Barbara Harmer would be regularly piloting an aircraft worth £107 million packed with celebrities across the Atlantic.

Barbara was born in Loughton, Epping Forest, Essex, in 1953 but soon moved to Bognor Regis, West Sussex. Her father was a commercial artist and her mother a haberdasher. Barbara was sent to a Catholic convent school and taught by nuns. She always described herself as a rebel even though she later admitted that the discipline she'd been taught

stood her in good stead during the years to come.

"If the nuns had known I was going to be a pilot they'd have said, 'Don't be so ridiculous'," she later recalled.

Although she was a successful hairdresser, young Barbara found herself feeling bored and unchallenged. Having stuck it out for five years, she resolved to improve the situation and got herself a position training to become an air traffic controller at Gatwick Airport. At the same time, she began studying to get some A-levels under her belt with the goal of eventually earning herself a law degree.

She said: "I just ordered the syllabuses from the examining boards, bought the

recommended texts and looked at past papers. I did it all by myself, with no tuition."

But the longer she spent around aircraft the more she wanted to take to the air herself. Gradually, her ambitious plan to enter the legal profession began to change. She started saving up every spare penny she could muster, £5000 in total, so she could pay for flying lessons and earn herself a pilot's licence. This wasn't enough so she took out a loan for another £10,000 to make it happen.

She took the controls of an aircraft, a Cessna, for the first time on December 26, 1975. Once she'd got the licence, she got a new job as a flying instructor at Goodwood Flying School. This though, was still not enough. Barbara's single minded

CHAPTER SEVEN

The French president's daughter-in-law

As the daughter of a wealthy shipbuilder, Jacqueline Auriol not only had a taste for action and adventure but also the means to go out and find it.

She married Paul Auriol, the son of Vincent Auriol, who served in France's highest office from 1947 to 1954, but quickly became famous in her own right.

Having qualified as a pilot in 1948, she challenged herself to achieve greater and greater feats of speed and aerial daring during the early 1950s.

She became the fastest woman in the world, flying a de Havilland Vampire jet, in May 1951 and went even faster later that year. She competed with her American friend Jacqueline Cochran to be the world's fastest woman and the title passed between them nine times as Auriol upgraded from one fast jet to the next, culminating in her achieving 1267mph in a Mirage IIIR in 1963. Cochran finally ended the contest in 1964 when she hit 1303mph in a two-seater TF-104G Starfighter.

Auriol piloted the first Concorde prototype, 001, in 1969. Her autobiography, published the following year, was entitled I Live To Fly. She died in 2000.

Jacqueline Auriol, who broke the women's air speed record in a Dassault Mystere jet fighter, was the first woman to fly Concorde.

David Beckham prepares to board Concorde, piloted by Barbara Harmer, with the Manchester United team. It was May 1999 ahead of their Champions League final match against Bayern Munich.

determination led her to spend two years studying for a commercial pilot's licence by correspondence course. She passed in May 1982.

Actually joining the world of civil aviation as a pilot was more difficult than she had imagined, however. She sent off application after application, only to have each one rejected in turn. All the while though, her experience as a pilot grew. Then, after more than 100 applications, she was successful. Genair, a small commuter airline that had recently relocated from Liverpool Airport to Humberside and forged close links with British Caledonian, took her on. During her time with the firm

she flew piston engined Embraer EMB 110 Bandeirantes and Short SD.330s.

Four months before Genair went into receivership in July 1984, Barbara moved on to British Caledonian where she had her first experience of jet airliners flying the BAC One-Eleven before moving on to the larger McDonnell Douglas DC-10. This lasted another four years before Caledonian merged with British Airways and Barbara had a new employer.

BA had nearly 3000 pilots on its books at the time but only 40 of them were women. The firm only started recruiting female pilots in 1987. Barbara was chosen for the intensive £100,000 six-month conversion course for

Concorde in 1992 – this time though she didn't have to pay for it herself. Now she was earning £37,000 a year – the equivalent of £64,000 today – with ambitions to become a captain earning £64,000 (£103,500).

Barbara made history on March 25, 1993, when she flew as first officer on a British Airways Concorde from London's Heathrow to JFK airport in New York. Not long after she'd begun regular flights she told an interviewer: "When you apply the power, you feel a nudge in your back and it goes off down the runway like a scalded cat. You can't believe the acceleration."

Flying at high altitude wasn't quite so exciting however: "Concorde is so smooth it doesn't really get the adrenalin going – but there's nothing else like it in the world. Even pilots stop and stare. It has an aura about it."

Barbara remained BA's only woman Concorde pilot to make regular flights for a decade, until October 2003 when it was withdrawn from regular commercial service, in the wake of the catastrophic accident to an Air France Concorde in July 2000.

During that time, her famous passengers included Mark Knopfler of Dire Straits, Eric Clapton, Sarah Brightman, Lord David Owen and Baroness Margaret Thatcher. Everything was fine for most of these journeys but Thatcher got a rough ride. Barbara later said: "She was travelling under an assumed name in Concorde back from New York in February. My landing at Heathrow was my worst ever. I thought, 'I hope they don't tell her it's a female at the controls. I'd hate her to think we can't cope'."

In May 1999 she flew the Manchester United squad to Barcelona to play Bayern Munichin the Champions League final. "I felt quite emotional as I taxied the Concorde out on to the runway," she remembered later, "with British flags flying and thousands of people wishing the team luck on the way."

In 2001, another woman, an Air France pilot named Béatrice Vialle, became the second female to fly Concorde on regular routes by making some 35 trips between Paris and New York before the service was finally withdrawn. Only one other woman flew Concorde, French test pilot Jacqueline Auriol, and then only during its development phase.

After Concorde, Barbara stayed on with BA, retraining to fly Boeing 777s until she took voluntary redundancy in 2009.

Flying fast jets wasn't Barbara's only passion however. She enjoyed driving fast cars, skiing, cycling long distance, gardening and playing tennis. She was even a fully qualified offshore yacht master and had planned to take part in a transatlantic event in her French-built 10.5m Archambault 35 in 2013. It was not to be however. She was diagnosed with ovarian cancer in 2009 and died at St Wilfrid's Hospice in Chichester on February 20, 2011, aged 57. A public memorial service was held at Chichester Cathedral.

The airports that welcomed Concorde (and those that didn't)

The sonic boom outcry that had killed off American attempts to create a supersonic airliner also made it difficult for Concorde to get a foothold in the US. A ban was imposed but once fears were allayed Concorde began to make its presence known at airports all over the world.

Having seen off the Boeing 2707, the American environmental lobby was not about to let another supersonic aircraft take to the skies over the US unopposed.

Beyond the problems associated with sonic booms, it was further suggested that Concorde's exhaust gases were more hazardous than those of other aircraft and that since it would fly closer to the ozone layer it would cause greater damage to it through chemical interactions.

It had always been intended that Concorde would fly from London and Paris to New York and the authorities there, where noise restrictions were imposed on airliners landing and taking off in the city, had taken a keen interest in the project from the outset.

As early as 1968, a year before even the first Concorde prototype had flown, the Port Authority of New York and New Jersey had approached manufacturers BAC and Sud Aviation and asked them for noise data on the aircraft. They had been told that as soon as data from flight testing was available it would be passed on.

During its early flight testing in 1969, Concorde stayed well clear of the US. It flew from its twin home bases of Filton, near Bristol, in Britain and Toulouse in southern France, making trips to RAF Fairford and Paris Le Bourget respectively. Other destinations close to home followed in 1970: Farnborough in Hampshire and London's

Getting permission for Concorde to land at New York's John F Kennedy Airport involved a tortuous and costly legal battle.
Tim Callaway

Heathrow Airport – where people living nearby complained about the noise.

Concorde was taken on its first trip beyond Europe on May 25, 1971, when 001 flew the 2500 miles from Paris to Dakar in Senegal, West Africa – a former French colony. Four months later, the same aircraft went on a tour of South America where it received a warm welcome at Rio de Janeiro having travelled there via the Cape Verde islands, Cayenne and Sao Paolo.

There was a visit to Germany for the Hanover Air Show by 002 in 1972 before the aircraft embarked on a demonstration tour to the east with destinations including Greece, Iran, Bahrain, India, Thailand, Singapore, Australia and Japan.

In his book, Concorde: The Inside Story, Brian Trubshaw described what it was like.

"First stop was Athens where the take off for Tehran was nothing short of frightening," he wrote. "Concorde did not relish the bumps and undulations of the runaway, which caused violent oscillations of the fuselage and flightdeck in particular. The pilots' headsets came off and I was shouting at the other pilot, Johnnie Walker, who was flying, to keep going in case he aborted the take off at too late a stage.

"This feature actually remained for the rest of the trip, especially at Bangkok and Singapore. At Tehran the thermal plus in the tyres blew necessitating a wheel change which prompted the Shah's personal bodyguard to demand an air test. This I refused and won the argument in exchange for a Concorde tie, pen and nearly one's shirt.

"The Shah flew next day and I was strapping him into the left-hand seat at Mach 2, when a large drop in outside air temperature occurred. The autopilot could not compete with the change and commenced a rapid climb following by an even more rapid descent during which air speed rose to 550 knots, 20 knots above the normal limit. However, the Shah was well pleased and indicated that Iran Air would purchase three Concordes following normal negotiations.

"Landing at Bombay outbound was peculiar because thousands of onlookers had broken lines and were jammed along each side of the runway. It was like landing on a football pitch.

"The next lesson was learned between Bombay and Bangkok. Concorde was predicted to fly above the weather in cloudless skies but this was not to be since Concorde was in a cloud at 60,000ft with tops going well above. Further temperature shears showed up the inadequacy of the autopilot to keep the aircraft within permitted speed limits.

"It was normal practice for overseas trips to be accompanied by a Government minister, Michael Heseltine and his wife covered the first part of the tour and were

US Secretary of Transportation William Coleman at a reception in New York City on Tuesday, January 21, 1975. Just over a year later the city's port authority would defy his decision to allow Concorde to operate a trial service from JFK airport.

replaced at Singapore by Lord and Lady Jellicoe. Mrs Heseltine became extremely poorly between Bombay and Bangkok but fortunately the services of Fred Clauson, a BOAC steward, saved the day with some oxygen in the decidedly primitive passenger cabin.

"Noise and smoke at Tokyo did not go down too well but landing in one direction and taking off in the opposite direction gave some alleviation on demonstration flights and on departure to Manila. Darwin produced the first bomb scare for Concorde from a mysterious telephone call in the middle of the night. As is so often the case, it was a complete hoax.

"A rapturous welcome occurred at Sydney, although the airfield fire brigade got rather excited when the tail bumper (fitted to prototypes) touched the runway and threw up a few sparks, which was perfectly normal. However, it encouraged a decision to fit a small wheel on the bumper of production aircraft. Visits to Melbourne and Adelaide all went very well with good serviceability and schedule keeping.

"The return part of the trip posed one particular problem on the Bangkok-Bombay sector where the only suitable alternative was Delhi. Fuel reserves were such that any decision to divert to Delhi had to be made before descent through 25,000ft. At this point the weather at Bombay was declared as wide open.

"However, at about 20 miles from Bombay with the aircraft now committed, it was quite obvious that the monsoon had arrived with a vengeance. 002 then entered cloud and we broke out at 400ft in very heavy rain, which made stopping after landing quite difficult but thanks to the tail parachute and reverse thrust there was

Concorde at Halifax Airport, Nova Scotia, Canada, on Wednesday, April 14, 1977.

plenty of runway left. A Boeing 707 following was not quite so lucky and went off the end.

"All this convinced me to chicken out of a planned demonstration flight and unserviceability was declared. This was the only flight including demonstrations at Teheran, Singapore, Tokyo, Sydney, Melbourne, Darwin, Dhahran and Beirut that was not completed to schedule. Heathrow was reached after a stopover at Toulouse with the Concorde 'antis' in full cry, although their efforts were somewhat spoiled by specially prepared postcards drawing attention to noise being posted 24 hours before we arrived."

Early the following year, 1973, 002 flew to Johannesburg in South Africa for hot weather testing and the French pre-production Concorde, 102, flew a 3728 mile nonstop round trip from Toulouse to Iceland and back – the equivalent distance of a Paris to New York flight. A month later, in March, 102 undertook a second distance demonstration – a 3900 mile flight from Toulouse to West Africa which was the same distance as a flight from Frankfurt to New York.

THE BATTLE FOR NEW YORK

There was further hot weather testing for 002 over Spain in July and Concorde finally crossed the Rubicon on September 20 when 102 flew from Paris to Dallas-Forth Worth for the new airport's dedication. The event was hosted by Braniff International Airways which, despite cancelling its option on three Concorde aircraft that March, still had

An Air France Concorde has ice hanging from its nose as it sits on the runway at Baltimore-Washington International Airport, near Linthicum, Maryland, Friday, on January 14, 1977. It had been diverted from Dulles due to poor weather. Concorde was still getting the cold shoulder from New York, however.

A security guard stands watch on the tower at Dulles International Airport in Washington, May 24, 1976, as Air France and British Airways Concorde aircraft park in front of the terminal. The pair had landed just minutes apart after flights from Paris and London – the first scheduled passengers services to America.

hopes of eventually using the aircraft to operate a Fort Worth-Washington-Paris service.

This visit brought Concorde's problems in the US into sharp relief. The primary stopper on regular services being operated between European airports and those in the America was the US National Environmental Policy Act of 1969, which President Richard Nixon had signed into law on January 1, 1970.

It set out a clear process that had to be followed whenever the US government wanted to consider a policy which might result in a major impact on the environment – such as allowing a regular supersonic airline service to operate from American airports.

This process was formally begun in February 1975 when British Airways and Air France sent letters to the Federal Aviation Administration (FAA) in Washington D. C. asking for permission to commence scheduled Concorde services to New York's John F Kennedy International Airport and Washington's Dulles International Airport in 1976.

An Environmental Impact Statement (EIS) had to be prepared by the FAA as evidence for the request and the Concorde team had already sent over a huge range of technical data to the FAA for this purpose in October 1974. The airlines had asked for only a limited commercial service, two flights every day to New York and one to

Washington, and the EIS was drawn up on this basis before being published for public scrutiny in March 1975.

There were well attended public hearings in New York, Washington and Virginia in April at which much vocal opposition and support for Concorde was expressed. The man who would decide whether to approve the supersonic service, Secretary of Transportation William Coleman, decided that a further public hearing would be held at Washington in January 1976.

Realising that this process was likely to take some time to conclude, British Airways and Air France began Concorde services

from London to Bahrain and Paris to Rio respectively on January 21.

During the January hearing in the US they insisted that "the limited environmental impact of a Concorde service to the United States will be far outweighed by the benefits of that service and by the important international considerations of technological progress and economic cooperation and harmony".

A month after the hearing Coleman agreed to allow a 16 month trial of up to two Concorde flights a day by each airline into New York and one a day by each into Washington. Flights could only take place between 7am and 10pm and supersonic

Bending the ozone layer

The American environmental campaigners who tried to keep Concorde out of the US used every means at their disposal to further their cause.

The aviation advisor at the British Embassy in Washington D. C., Sandy Gordon-Cumming, said: "One entire class in a school near Kennedy, 9- or 10-year-olds, wrote to me individually at the bidding of their teacher. They all wrote clearly at their teacher's

dictation, and she was not a very scientific lady because one of the things they alleged Concorde would do was to bend the ozone layer. I took great pleasure in writing back to them individually, enclosing a Concorde poster, and the biggest poster went to a little lad called Matthew, aged 8.

"He wrote down all the stuff his teacher had dictated, then he had the guts to add: 'But I hope it will come'. He got a set of photographs as well."

flight would not be allowed over US soil. The FAA had decided that Concorde met all the relevant safety requirements but Coleman was still concerned that Concorde might be too noisy and might have a negative long term impact on the environment – evidence about which was still lacking.

Some of environmental campaigners had even argued that the aircraft should be banned outright as a purely symbolic gesture regarding its lack of fuel efficiency but Coleman dismissed this idea saying: "It would be unfair to single out the Concorde as an appropriate symbol of US fuel conservation policy. We did not build it. We will not pay its fuel bills. It would border on hypocrisy to choose the Concorde as the place to set an example, while ignoring the relative inefficiency of private jets, cabin cruisers or an assortment of energy profligates of American manufacture."

Getting the trial going at Dulles was easy since the FAA ran it and Coleman's Department of Transportation ran the FAA. New York was different. The city's port authority had continued to watch the progress of Concorde carefully since its initial approach to BAC and Sud Aviation in 1968 – eight years earlier. Now it was being told by the Federal Government that it had to accept Concorde flights and this rankled. So in March 1976, a month after Coleman's trial was announced, it passed legislation banning Concorde from the city.

BA and Air France launched a legal battle against the port authority and the authority countered by ordering a six month study of noise produced by Concorde flights between Europe and Dulles, which began on May 24.

The port authority's six months came and went and still the ban remained so in February 1977 British Prime Minister James Callaghan and President Valéry Giscard d'Estaing of France wrote personal letters to President Jimmy Carter on the subject.

Carter, who had been in office for less than a month and had spoken out against

A traditional Chinese lion dance is being performed for the benefit of Concorde passengers after the inaugural flight from London to Singapore arrived on December 10, 1977.

Concorde during his election campaign, said he could not direct the port authority to reach a particular decision.

In May, Judge Milton Pollack in the Federal District Court ruled that the port authority's ban on Concorde flights was illegal because it went against Coleman's federal ruling. The authority fended this off by lodging an appeal which was upheld. Pollack made the same ruling of an illegal ban again on August 17 after the case came back to him and noted that the authority had been "discriminatory, arbitrary and unreasonable".

The port authority lodged yet another appeal but this was rejected and the appeals court ruled that the ban, having now been in place for 19 months, should be ended immediately. Even then, the port authority tried to keep its challenge alive by taking it to the US Supreme Court but the court declined to get involved in the case.

Concorde services to John F Kennedy International Airport commenced on November 22, 1977, and monitoring equipment confirmed right from the outset

that it complied with New York's own restrictions on noise.

Coleman's 16 month trial period at Dulles demonstrated that Concorde was twice as noisy as the noisiest subsonic jet on takeoff and approach but air quality was less affected than had been anticipated. A total of 1387 complaints were received.

During the 12 months after Concorde's first flight to New York, 3694 complaints were received. American type approval for Concorde to operate in the US was finally granted in January 1979.

Since then, Concorde has visited more than 300 destinations in 108 different countries.

BRANIFF'S US SERVICES AND SINGAPORE AIRLINES
While the legal battle for permission to land in New York raged, Air France and British Airways continued to look for alternative long distance Concorde routes. In particular, it was hoped that it could be used for services in Asia or on the 'Kangaroo Routes' to Australia.

French President Valéry Giscard D'Estaing arrives at Haneda Airport, Tokyo, on June 27, 1979, aboard Concorde to attend a two day summit.

British and French Concorde aircraft pass each other on the runway after landing at New York's JFK Airport for the first time on Tuesday, November 22, 1977. The city had just lost a bitter legal battle to keep them out.

Services to Bahrain had begun in 1976 but much of this had been overland and the aircraft had been forced to fly at subsonic speeds. Faster than sound flights over Saudi Arabia had been ended after nomads claimed sonic booms were discouraging their camels from breeding.

After much negotiation, on October 26, 1977, British Airways was able to announce that it had reached an agreement with Singapore Airlines for a three-times-a-week Concorde service to Singapore from London via Bahrain. The route's assigned aircraft, G-BOAD, was repainted with Singapore Airlines livery down its left side. The right side retained its BA paint scheme.

The first flight was on December 9, 1977, and it took nine hours even avoiding India, which had refused permission for access to its airspace. The pilot and crew were British and so were half the flight attendants – but the rest were from Singapore.

After just three return flights the service had to be brought to a premature end due after the Malaysian government complained about the noise. A new route avoiding the country was plotted and flights resumed on January 24, 1979.

London to Singapore Concorde flights finally came to an end on November 1, 1980, due to falling passenger numbers on the route which was resulting in an annual loss

of around £2 million. Just as the Singapore route was restarting however, another international route was also being established. Concorde was now type certified for the US and America's Braniff International Airways was in a position to fulfil its desire to use the aircraft. It established a Fort Worth-Dulles-London/Paris flight schedule using Concorde supplied by Air France and British Airways.

The American leg was flown by Braniff's own pilots and crew before the British and French crews took over for the remainder of the journey. It went further than this though. Actual ownership of the aircraft was transferred to Braniff but only during the American flight.

In the US, the G and F registration numbers were covered with tape and American registrations were displayed to reflect their ownership.

For insurance reasons, a BA captain and flight engineer had to sit in the cockpit to observe the American flight crews at work. A total of 14 Braniff personnel were trained to operate Concorde – three pilots, five co-pilots, four flight engineers, a check pilot and a check engineer.

Services commenced with British Airways' G-BOAE and Air France's F-BTSD on January 12, 1979, but operating costs were higher than passenger numbers could support and Braniff's ambitious international Concorde service came to an end in May 1980.

Concorde on the runway at JFK airport in New York City on June 18, 1981. By now the city had largely forgotten its earlier animosity towards the aircraft.

Concorde around the world

Destinations for regular, charter and other flights 1976 to 2003

1. **Antigua and Barbuda:**
St John's

2. **Argentina:**
Buenos Aires
Peuro Iguazu

3. **Australia:**
Brisbane
Darwin
Learmonth
Perth
Sydney

4. **Austria:**
Graz
Klagenfurt
Linz
Salzburg
Vienna

5. **Bahamas:**
Nassau

6. **Bahrain:**
Muharraq

7. **Bangladesh:**
Dacca

8. **Barbados:**
Seawell

9. **Belgium:**
Brussels
Charleroi
Liège
Ostend

10. **Bermuda:**
Hamilton

11. **Brazil:**
Barreirinhas
Brasilia
Recife

12. **Burkina Faso:**
Ouagadougou

13. **Burundi:**
Bujumbura

14. **Cameroon:**
Douala

15. **Canada:**
Calgary
Edmonton
Gander (diversion only)
Goose Bay
Halifax (diversion only)
Moncton
Montreal
Ottawa
Quebec
Regina

16. **Cayman Islands:**
Grand Cayman

17. **Central African Republic:**
Bangui

18. **Colombia:**
Bogota
Cartagena

19. **Cuba:**
Havana

20. **Cyprus:**
Larnaca

21. **Czech Republic:**
Prague

22. **Democratic Republic of Congo:**
Kinshasa

23. **Denmark:**
Aarhus
Aalborg
Billund
Copenhagen

24. **Djibouti:**
Djibouti City

25. **Easter Island:**
Hanga Roa

26. **Egypt:**
Aswan
Cairo
Luxor

27. **Fiji:**
Nadi

28. **Finland:**
Helsinki
Ivalo
Rovaniemi
Turku

29. **France:**
Bastia
Beauvais
Biarritz
Bordeaux
Brest
Cambrai
Chateauroux
Clermont-Ferrand
Dijon
Epinal
Grenoble
Lille
Lyon
Marseille
Metz
Montpellier
Mulhouse
Nantes
Nice
Paris CDG
Paris Orly
Paris Le Bourget
Poitiers
Reims
Strasbourg
Tarbes
Toulouse
Tours
Vichy

30. **French Guiana:**
Cayenne

31. **French Polynesia:**
Papeete
Hao
Mururoa

32. **Gabon:**
Libreville

33. **Germany:**
Berlin
Frankfurt
Hamburg
Cologne
Hanover
Leipzig
Munich
Nuremberg

34. **Greece:**
Athens

35. **Greenland:**
Kangerlussuaq (Sondrestrom)

36. **Grenada:**
St George's

37. **Guadeloupe:**
Pointe-a-Pitre

38. **Guam:**
Hagatna

39. **Guinea:**
Conakry

40. **Haiti:**
Port-au-Prince

41. **Hong Kong:**
Kai Tak

42. **Hungary:**
Budapest

43. **Iceland:**
Keflavik

44. **India:**
Bombay
Calcutta
Delhi
Madras
Patna

45. **Indonesia:**
Denpasar
Jakarta

46. **Iran:**
Kish
Tehran

47. **Ireland:**
Dublin
Munster
Shannon (diversion only)

48. **Israel:**
Haifa
Tel Aviv

49. **Italy:**
Ancona
Bologna
Milan Linate
Milan Malpensa
Pescara
Pisa
Rome Fiumicino
Turin
Venice

50. **Ivory Coast:**
Abidjan
Yamoussoukro

51. **Jamaica:**
Kingston
Montego Bay

52. **Japan:**
Nagasaki
Osaka/Kansai
Tokyo

53. **Jordan:**
Amman
Aqaba

54. **Kenya:**
Mombasa
Nairobi

55. **Kingdom of the Netherlands:**
Aruba

56. **Kuwait:**
Kuwait City

57. **Lebanon:**
Beirut

58. **Liberia:**
Robertsfield (Monrovia)

59. **Luxembourg:**
Luxembourg City

60. **Madagascar:**
Antananrivo

61. **Malaysia:**
Kuala Lumpur

62. **Mali:**
Bamako

63. **Malta:**
Luqa

64. **Martinique:**
Fort-de-France

65. **Mauritius:**
Grand Port

66. **Mexico:**
Acapulco
Mexico City

67. **Morocco:**
Agadir
Casablanca
Marrakesh
Tangier

68. **Nepal:**
Kathmandu

69. **Netherlands:**
Amsterdam

70. **New Caledonia:**
Nouméa

71. **New Zealand:**
Auckland
Christchurch

72. **Nigeria:**
Lagos

73. **Norway:**
Bergen
Oslo
Stavanger

74. **Oman:**
Muscat

75. **Pakistan:**
Islamabad

76. **Peru:**
Lima

77. **Poland:**
Warsaw

78. **Portugal:**
Faro
Lajes Field
Lisbon
Oporto

79. **Puerto Rico:**
San Juan

80. **Republic of Trinidad and Tobago:**
Port of Spain

81. **Réunion:**
Saint-Denis

82. **Russia:**
Baikonur
Moscow
Novosibirsk
St Petersburg

83. **Rwanda:**
Kigali

84. **Saudi Arabia:**
Dhahran
Jeddah
Riyadh

85. **Senegal:**
Dakar

86. **Seychelles:**
Mahé

87. **Singapore:**
Changi

88. **Slovakia:**
Bratislava

89. **South Africa:**
Cape Town
Johannesburg

90. **Spain:**
Albacete
Ibiza
Badajoz
Barcelona
Lanzarote
Las Palmas
Madrid
Malaga
Santiago de Compostela

91. **Sri Lanka:**
Colombo

92. **Sweden:**
Gothenburg
Stockholm
Vasteras

93. **Switzerland:**
Basel
Geneva

94. **Tanzania:**
Kilimanjaro (Hai District)

95. **Thailand:**
Bangkok
Chiang Mai

96. **Togo:**
Lome

97. **Tunisia:**
Djerba
Tozeur
Tunis

98. **Turkey:**
Ankara
Istanbul

99. **Union of Comoros:**
Moroni

100. **United Arab Emirates:**
Abu Dhabi
Dubai

101. **United Kingdom:**
Aberdeen
Belfast
Birmingham
Boscombe Down
Bournemouth
Brize Norton
Cardiff
Coltishall
Derby
East Midlands
Edinburgh
Exeter
Fairford
Farnborough
Filton
Finningley
Gatwick
Glasgow
Hatfield
Heathrow
Humberside
Kinloss
Leeds
Leuchars
Liverpool
Llanbedr
Luton
Macrihanish
Manchester
Manston
Mildenhall
Newcastle
Prestwick
St Mawgan
Stansted
Teeside
Yeovilton

102. **United States of America:**
Abbotsford
Albany
Andrews AFB
Anchorage
Asheville
Atlanta
Atlantic City
Austin (Texas)
Baltimore
Bangor
Battle Creek
Boston
Buffalo
Charleston
Chicago
Cincinnati
Cleveland
Colorado Springs
Columbus
Dayton
Denver
Detroit
Fort Lauderdale
Fort Myers
Hampton
Harrisburg
Hartford/ Springfield
Honolulu
Houston Ellington
Houston
International
Indianapolis
Jackson
Jacksonville
Kailua-Kona
Kansas City
Las Vegas
Lexington
Little Rock
Lubbock
Miami
Midland-Odessa
Nashville
Newark (diversion only)
Newburg Stewart
New Orleans
Newport
New York
Oakland
Oklahoma City
Omaha
Ontario (USA)
Orlando
Oshkosh
Philadelphia
Phoenix
Pittsburgh
Portland
Providence
Raleigh
Windsor Locks (diversion only)

103. **Uruguay:**
Montevideo

104. **Uzbekistan:**
Tashkent

105. **Venezuela:**
Caracas

106. **Yemen:**
Sana'a

107. **Zambia:**
Lusaka

108. **Zimbabwe:**
Harare

Smiles in the air
Concorde's cabin crew

Working as a flight attendant on board Concorde brought prestige and a unique opportunity to meet the rich and famous. It also meant working within the aircraft's tiny galleys and learning to move quickly up and down its narrow central aisle.

Concorde's key selling point, besides its supersonic speed, was the luxury service it offered for every passenger. This was provided by a cabin crew of six including the cabin services director and a purser.

Joining Concorde was an optional two year secondment for British Airways cabin crew, who were able to put their name down for a fleet change every two years. Applicants were interviewed and had to undergo a personnel file review and assuming these were both satisfactory places were allocated on a seniority within

rank basis. Concorde crew were not exclusive to the aircraft, being also expected to work on board other narrow bodied aircraft such as Boeing 757s and Airbus A319/320s.

Air France adopted a different approach, holding internal recruitment sessions. Cabin crew who wanted to apply had to have been with the airline for a minimum of three years and had to speak good English, good being defined as a 'four' on a scale of five in the language. They also had to speak a third language and their personnel record needed to be clean since it was reviewed several times during the recruitment process. If the

file was up to scratch and the candidate's years in service could be regarded as exemplary they reached the interview stage. Beyond this, crew were given training on the aircraft itself including safety protocol and given additional service training.

French crews also divided their work between Concorde and other aircraft although these were long haul types such as Airbus A330s, Boeing 777s and Boeing 747s.

Both airlines placed an emphasis on rapid, inobtrusive, personal service. If a passenger asked for a drink, the attendant would ideally stop what they were doing and go to fetch it. They also seldom had time to

ABOVE: Flight attendants Louise Brown (left) and Laurence Ricaul prepare to pour the bubbly for Concorde passengers.

LEFT: Dawn Maskrey makes final safety and security checks ahead of Concorde's first commercial crossing of the Atlantic since the fleet was grounded for modifications in 2000.

OPPOSITE: Cabin crew serve refreshments to passengers aboard a British Airways Concorde.

take a break and were frequently called upon to take passengers' photos for them in addition to serving the drinks and food.

Flight attendant Sally Armstrong, from Barton on Sea in Hampshire, joined the crew of Concorde in 1980 and met numerous celebrities during her time on the aircraft. Among them were Robert de Niro, David Attenborough, Tom Cruise, John McEnroe, Mick Jagger and Jerry Hall, Estee Lauder, David Frost and Ringo Starr.

On one flight she met Elizabeth Taylor and later recalled: "She was between husbands. She was one of the icons I'd always wanted to meet. She sat in the front cabin, so there was no-one behind her. On the other side was Michael Douglas with a starlet.

"My friend Bernadette said: 'Just go and look at Liz Taylor's eyes'. I took her drink down for her – she was looking at me, so I didn't want to stare too much. She was so beautiful. Bernadette came up to her and they were chatting away. She said: 'Miss Taylor, your ring is so beautiful'. Miss Taylor slipped it off her finger and said: 'Just try it on, honey'."

She said she had taken the ring to the toilets with her friend and they each tried it on.

"We were afraid we were going to drop it down the loo," she said. "We weren't long – we were in the middle of a meal service. It was one of those lovely moments."

She also vividly remembered a conversation with American movie actress Claudette Colbert: "She was in her eighties and would have a glass of champagne. I asked: 'Is that the secret of your long life?' She said: 'Yes – and living in Barbados'.

She said country music singer Dolly Parton had been "stunning, bright, friendly", and singer John Denver had a "beautiful smile".

Another flight attendant, Tracey Percy, said: "Richard Gere was one of our favourites. You would ask a question and he takes off his glasses and closes his book and looks at you and asks you what the question was – and by the time he has done that you have forgotten what it was yourself."

Concorde's cabin crew were frequently its unsung heroes, their skill and friendly devotion to duty were essential to the supersonic airliner's success.

CHAPTER TEN

Flying on board Concorde

First class travel beyond the sound barrier

Booking your tickets for a flight aboard Concorde wasn't cheap whenever you flew during its 27 years in service but your money bought you an experience unlike any other. It was the journey of a lifetime no matter how many times you made it.

Nobody flew second class with Concorde. The entire experience was one of luxury living no matter who you were. Let us book into a typical flight from Heathrow to New York – without having to pay for the ticket.

At Heathrow, the special Concorde Room was probably the best in the world with a great selection of food, drinks and seating, which was an indication of the super flight ahead. Many passengers took advantage of the complimentary treatments and showers at the Molton Brown Travel Spa.

The Concorde Room had comfortable seating with leather chairs, small tables, and telephones, which were scattered about the lounge, occasionally divided by small partitions. Although the lounge was usually busy it was rare to find anyone having trouble locating a place to sit.

The bar in Heathrow's Concorde Room offered a comprehensive menu from which passengers could order complimentary sandwiches, salads, and other made-to-order dishes, as well as a wide variety of drinks. You name it, you could have it, whether hot or cold, alcoholic or alcohol-free.

Business travellers were far from neglected as there were work desks available, two of which offered PC terminals with complimentary internet access. There was also a full service business centre next to the Concorde Room.

It sounds good already, but that is still not the end of it as the Concorde Room and Lounge Pavilion at London Heathrow included a fully staffed luggage and coat desk for storing cumbersome items while enjoying the lounge.

What about the Molton Brown Travel Spa? That was on the lower level of the Lounge Pavilion and offered a variety of different 20 minute complimentary treatments, including back, facial and foot massage. By now, the less seasoned traveller might easily be thinking that this was enough, without even actually setting foot on the aircraft and leaving the ground. However, all this was just a sample of what was to come.

ABOVE: Once inside the Concorde Room, two more BA staff members greet passengers and check boarding cards. Nathan Roemer

LEFT: Gateway to the ultimate luxury experience. Outside the Concorde Room entrance a BA staff member waits to direct First and Club World passengers to their respective lounges. Nathan Roemer

ABOVE: Comfy leather seats, small tables and glass partitions in the Concorde passenger lounge. Nathan Roemer

ABOVE RIGHT: The main corridor connecting the business centre, visible in the distance, with the bar. Nathan Roemer

RIGHT: Light dining before takeoff – freshly prepared prawn sandwiches with crisps, a Coke and a Schweppes Bitter Lemon from the bar. Nathan Roemer

At last, the boarding announcements gently invited passengers to gather their belongings and go through the glass doors at the far end of the lounge to board Concorde. The excitement is now building. Those who have flown before try to appear fairly nonchalant, some of those who have never flown before also try to keep the look of an experienced traveller, while others are totally honest and make no attempt to conceal their delight as the big moment arrives and they are met and greeted by the immaculate and welcoming cabin crew.

One of the first things most people noticed upon entering the aircraft was its narrow fuselage, low ceiling, and elongated galleys. Seats were in pairs with 25 rows of four seats separated into two cabins: there were 10 rows in the forward cabin, and 15 rows in the rear, or aft, cabin. The rows were numbered 1 to 26 with row 13 omitted… for some reason. Concorde was certainly very different to most long-haul planes with their wide bodies – Concorde was a rocket with wings.

Once they had found their seat, most passengers took advantage of the small overhead lockers before making themselves comfortable for the flight ahead. Cabin staff kept a watchful eye on passengers, ready to help with the stowing of belongings in the lockers or indeed in the valet closets elsewhere in the plane.

Most passengers relaxing on Concorde for the first time quickly realised how

small the windows were, but differences like this only added to the experience, rather than detract from it. Suddenly, you begin to feel more like an astronaut than an airline passenger.

The atmosphere on board Concorde was always party-like. The Concorde Room at Heathrow was always animated. The first-timers were excited and even those who had flown before knew they were about to relive an amazing experience. As people settled in, quite a few would start taking photographs and chat to fellow passengers about this being their first time, or that they were taking the flight in celebration of an anniversary or some other special event in their lives, or perhaps even fulfilling a dream. It was nice that the cabin and flight crew were all caught up in the excitement as well, sharing the experience by volunteering to take photos for passengers, talking about the flight, or how much they loved working on Concorde. The surroundings were plush. Just about everything reminded you that you were on

British Airways' Concorde, with logos on the seatbelt buckles and the backs of the seat headrests, not to mention the drink glasses and mats, which were soon to come. The party was under way. Flying Concorde was never dull.

There was another buzz of excitement as the great aircraft began to taxi to its allocated runway. During the taxi, the captain introduced himself and made a few announcements about the flying time, the weather and how the Concorde take-off was unlike any other. At the same time, the flight attendants passed through the cabin to take in-flight drink orders and provide a hot-towel service.

The next big moment, and possibly the greatest, soon arrived. The aircraft steadily came to a halt on its starting blocks and the anticipation of passengers grew even higher. Suddenly the plane was on its way to an exhilarating take-off. The afterburners were switched on and Concorde raced across the Tarmac at a much higher speed than other aircraft, passengers slightly

ABOVE: Tasteful art on the walls, exotic flowers on the tables and plenty of reading material on tap at the bar. Nathan Roemer

LEFT: Concorde's ground facilities offered ample facilities for the business traveller such as desks to work on and full internet access, even in 2003. Nathan Roemer

BELOW: The moodily lit upper floor of the British Airways Lounge Pavilion. Nathan Roemer

pressed against their seats. Excitement mounted even more and finally the wheels left the ground. Once in the air, the afterburners were cut, and there was a significantly noticeable reduction in noise and thrust as the aircraft flew onwards and upwards.

A few minutes into the flight, the cabin information displays were activated and the next phase in this great experience began. Within a very short space of time Concorde was flying over the Atlantic and the captain announced that clearance had been given to switch on the afterburners for a second time to achieve supersonic speed. He explained that the afterburners would be switched on in pairs and passengers could expect to feel two bits of extra thrust when this happened. At an altitude of just under 28,000ft, the great aircraft broke the sound barrier and achieved Mach 1.

Once into supersonic mode, the flight attendants passed through the cabin to distribute menus for brunch and to serve the previously ordered drinks, along with

champagne and canapés. The menus were quite stylish – blue embossed card stock covers and heavyweight paper pages bound with a blue binding string fastened with a silver ball.

One of the disadvantages of a much shorter journey time is the cramming in of meals and drinks serving. However, the cabin crew remained unfazed and the meal service was always friendly and efficient. The smiles never dropped and, amazingly, always looked genuine, and there was never a shortage of spare chocolates, either.

Yes, some of the utensils, complying to safety issues, were plastic, but with bone china plates, silver napkin rings, and very smart salt and pepper grinders, who was complaining?

Soon after champagne service, passengers heard from the captain again who explained that Concorde was now travelling at its maximum cruise speed of Mach 2, twice the speed of sound. Around about now passengers were also told that the aircraft was cruising at an altitude

ABOVE RIGHT: Even amid the finery of the travel spa, passengers could still keep a watchful eye on departure times. Nathan Roemer

TOP: Prepare to be pampered – British Airways Molton Brown Travel Spa. Nathan Roemer

ABOVE: Passengers could take a load off and relax prior to their flight. Nathan Roemer

ABOVE: Travel can be a sweaty, grimy business but help was on hand. Nathan Roemer

LEFT: Spa shower suite; toilet and shower. Nathan Roemer

BELOW: A Concorde Lounge flight information board listing flight BA 001 for New York. Nathan Roemer

between 55-60,000ft – far above the weather, allowing for an extremely smooth, turbulence-free flight. Indeed, at this high altitude, the sky could be seen to be a deep indigo blue and the view through the small windows was totally remarkable.

Talking of the windows, passengers could not fail to notice that those windows were very warm to the touch. Despite the freezing temperature of the air outside, Concorde's airframe actually became very hot due to the friction of the air passing over the plane at supersonic speeds. This not only served to cause the windows to feel surprisingly warm from the inside, but it also caused Concorde to stretch in length more than 6in during its flight.

Looking out of the windows, passengers also had the amazing experience of identifying the gradual curve of the earth below, a sight which became even more evident when viewed from nearer the centre of the cabin and seen through several windows at once.

During the final stages of the flight, cabin crew fulfilled the time-honoured task of offering items for sale from the duty free catalogue. There were several Concorde items featured in the catalogue that were very popular among passengers. There was also a mail order service for anyone who wanted something that was out of stock or for which they did not have the payment at the time.

The first indication that the flight was nearing its end was a very noticeable deceleration, which could be felt quite plainly by the passengers. This was followed by an announcement from the captain that the aircraft was approaching its destination and would be slowing to subsonic speed once again. Not only was the flight so much quicker than in any other aircraft, but the unique experience also meant that time seemed to pass so much more quickly. No sooner had the first champagne glass been raised than it was almost time to prepare to land. The bulkhead information display

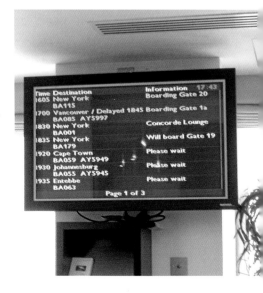

ABOVE: Concorde is prepared for take-off – not long now. Nathan Roemer

ABOVE LEFT: Your carriage awaits. These doors led directly to the Concorde boarding ramp. Nathan Roemer

LEFT: The voyage begins as Concorde leaves the runway at London's Heathrow airport.

BELOW: The sight every passenger wanted to see – Mach 2 indicated on the in-cabin display. Commercial travellers haven't gone that fast for nearly a decade now.

It's all over. Concorde touches down after a successful flight.

indicated the much slower speed of the plane and the start of the descent. For many, this was the time they least looked forward to – it was not a fear of landing, but the fact that the whole experience was nearing its end.

As the ground crept up from below, the bulkhead cabin displays switched to a very simple 'Thank-you for flying Concorde'. Within a few moments, the landing gear was lowered into position and condensation began to rush over the wings. The landing was very graceful as Concorde glided down to earth for a smooth touchdown. Once on the ground, the captain threw the reverse thrusters into gear and gradually brought the flying machine down to taxi speed.

Most left the plane with a buzz of conversation, clutching their hand luggage, and once the jetty was in position, everyone gathered their belongings and souvenir flight certificates and said farewell to the flight and cabin crew, who all looked as fresh as when they had first welcomed everyone aboard.

That still wasn't quite the end of the experience as Concorde passengers landing at Heathrow were invited to use fast-track immigration services. The VIP treatment was not quite over until passengers were safely reunited with their luggage and were on their way home or to their hotel, still dazed by their experience and now totally in love with Concorde.

The British Airways Concorde fleet is united at Heathrow Airport to celebrate the aircraft's 10th anniversary in service in January 1986.

Concorde's magical moments

Milestones and special occasions

During its time in British Airways service it was said that Concorde accounted for only 2-3% of the firm's overall fleet capacity but took up about 30% of managers' time. It was an aircraft bound up with British and French national prestige in a way like no other and as much as it was reserved as a special treat for others it was on the receiving end of plenty of special treatment itself as it passed one important milestone after the next.

CHAPTER ELEVEN

Concorde's first British test pilot Brian Trubshaw (right) at Filton, near Bristol, with British Airways chief Concorde pilot Captain Mike Bannister in 1999, 30 years to the day after the first aircraft of its type made its maiden flight from Filton to Fairford.

André Turcat, French Concorde's chief test pilot, said that when the aircraft was rolled out for the first time it was to him like the birth of his son, a special occasion which mere words could not describe.

But this was only the beginning, the first of many special Concorde occasions that would be celebrated during its long and distinguished career. There was to follow the first flight, the first flight to another country, the first supersonic flight, and many other 'firsts' that would grab newspaper headlines every time.

A number of Concorde's special flights took place in conjunction with the Red Arrows aerobatic display team. It first flew with the Arrows in 1973 when it was still using Folland Gnat jet trainers. The aircraft chosen was G-AXDN, the British pre-production version, and since the display team was based at RAF Kemble, not far from RAF Fairford where 101 was based at the time, it seemed like an ideal opportunity to fly two of Britain's most popular aviation icons together.

Also in 1973, on June 30, a team of scientists from Britain, France and America used F-WTSS to study a solar eclipse that was expected to be the longest seen for more than 1000 years. The aircraft's speed as it flew from Las Palmas in the Canaries Islands to Fort Lamy, Chad, at 55,000ft made the eclipse continuously visible for 80 minutes.

The following year Concorde successfully clocked up a total of 3000 hours of flight testing and 1000 hours of flying at supersonic speeds and G-AXDN made the fastest ever east-west crossing of the North Atlantic by an airliner on November 7, by flying from Fairford to Bangor, Maine, US, in just two hours and 56 minutes.

There was further testing and prolonged court action in 1975 and 1976 as British Airways (BA) and Air France built up their respective fleets and began the first scheduled services to the US – though to Washington only.

On May 21, 1977, to mark the 50th anniversary of Charles Lindbergh's flight in his Spirit of St Louis aircraft from New York to Paris, a Concorde flew the same route, completing the flight in three hours and 44 minutes compared to Lindbergh's time of 33 hours 29 minutes.

There were celebrations to mark Concorde's second anniversary in commercial service on January 21, 1978, when the aircraft was calculated to have already carried more than 129,000 passengers. BA alone carried its 100,000th Concorde passenger on August 10 of that year.

By January 21 the following year, Concorde had carried nearly 300,000 passengers and accumulated a total of 21,700 hours in the air.

Concorde took to the skies with the Red Arrows again in 1980. G-BBDG, the British

production test Concorde, had its BA logos removed and then linked up with the Red Arrows display team flying their new British Aerospace Hawk trainer jets for a formation photo opportunity.

More than 700,000 passengers had travelled by Concorde as of January 21, 1981, and the aircraft had completed 15,800 flights with a grand total of 50,000 flying hours.

There was trouble brewing during the same year however, and the future of Concorde appeared uncertain. In April, a report published by the Commons Industry and Trade Committee expressed dissatisfaction with the cost figures and recommended that more effort should be made to ensure the costs were shared equally with France. Then, in July, the British Government replied to the report, describing its criticisms as "unwarranted".

An Anglo-French summit meeting was held and the British and French governments commissioned a joint study to look at the aircraft's potential to continue as a commercial airliner. In late October, British and French ministers met again in London and this time they came up with three proposals: the cancellation of the Concorde project; a phased run-down of the project; or indefinite continuation. In early December, the British government reviewed the relative costs of Concorde presented to it by the Department of Industry.

It was accepted that the British Government had lost money on Concorde

Concorde leads the RAF's Red Arrows display team as they fly over Heathrow Airport on June 2, 1996, to celebrate its 50th anniversary.

during every year of its operation – although this was not an unexpected finding since the cost of developing Concorde in the first place had been colossal and there had been no 'customer' airlines to help recoup the initial outlay.

Nevertheless, serious consideration was given to the possibility of withdrawing the aircraft from service. In May 1982 British and French ministers met in Paris and discussed cost reduction measures and cost sharing. This was followed in August by Conservative junior trade minister Iain Sproat writing officially to BA chairman Sir John King stating that the British Government was planning to end Government funding of Concorde's British manufacturers Rolls-Royce and British Aerospace.

King replied in October, stating that BA would examine the possibility of funding the support costs of Concorde out of its own revenue and within a matter of weeks BA

had set up a group to examine the costs associated with supporting Concorde. There were ongoing discussions at this time about the possibility of privatising BA, which would remain state owned until 1987.

The uncertainty about Concorde continued but in 1983 King convinced the Government to sell BA its seven Concorde aircraft outright for £16.5 million plus the first year's profits. King recognised that, in Concorde, BA had a premier product that was under-priced. Market research had revealed that many customers believed Concorde was more expensive than it actually was; therefore ticket prices were raised to match those perceptions. It is reported that BA then managed to successfully run Concorde at a profit, unlike its French counterpart.

Concorde continued to prove it was the finest luxury airliner in service on April 25, 1985, when BA Concorde G-BOAG was used to showed off the fleet's new interior

furnishings and exterior livery. The same aircraft then put in a memorable appearance at the Royal International Air Tattoo, flying in formation with the Red Arrows again and this time linking up with the QE2 as well during a flight over the English Channel.

To mark a decade of commercial service on January 21, 1986, BA flew four aircraft – G-BOAA, G-BOAB, G-BOAC and G-BOAG – in formation over the Atlantic. Between them, the British and French aircraft had now achieved 71,000 supersonic flying hours.

There was another stunning record between November 8-23, 1986, when Concorde made its first round the world charter flight. The total flying time amounted to 31 hours 51 minutes. It was such a success that a second round the world flight was made the following year.

On October 5, 1987, Patrick Mannix, of news agency Reuters, became British Airways' one millionth transatlantic

TOP: French test pilot Andre Turcat, left, and his British counterpart Brian Trubshaw hold brightly painted models of the British/French supersonic Concorde aircraft in front of the aircraft's 20th anniversary cake in Toulouse on March 2, 1989.

ABOVE: Concorde itself goes psychedelic for its 20th birthday in Toulouse.

scheduled Concorde passenger and then, on November 22, Concorde celebrated its 10th anniversary of operations into John F Kennedy International Airport, New York, with Richard Noble, the then land speed record holder, setting a new record by crossing the Atlantic three times in one day aboard Concorde.

G-BOAA became the first Concorde to require a 12,000 flying hours check in April 1988. It passed the exhaustive test with flying colours and engineers reported that the aircraft's structure would be sound for continued service until well into the 21st century.

On March 2, 1989, French manufacturer Aérospatiale hosted a party to celebrate the 20th anniversary of Concorde's first flight from Toulouse. The idea for the event came from tour operator Goodwood Travel which hired two Concorde aircraft, one from BA and one from Air France, to ferry 200

guests, including test pilot Brian Trubshaw, from Heathrow to the Aérospatiale facility where the French production test Concorde, F-WTSB or 201, was on display.

Aérospatiale itself invited still more guests to the event and invited local artists to give the aircraft a unique psychedelic red white and blue colour scheme. Trubshaw gave two speeches, one to the French guests and one to the Goodwood Travel group, and brought French test pilot André Turcat into the proceedings too. He also gave a short speech.

There were very many record-breaking moments for Concorde. It set the official FAI westbound around the world and eastbound around the world air speed records. On October 12-13, 1992, in commemoration of the 500th anniversary of Columbus' first New World landing, Concorde Spirit Tours (USA) chartered Air France Concorde F-BTSD and circumnavigated the world in 32

hours 49 minutes three seconds from Lisbon, including six refuelling stops at Santo Domingo, Acapulco, Honolulu, Guam, Bangkok, and Bahrain.

The eastbound record was set by the same Air France Concorde under charter to Concorde Spirit Tours on August 15-16, 1995. This was a promotional flight and circumnavigated the world from New York/JFK International Airport in 31 hours 27 minutes 49 seconds, including six refuelling stops at Toulouse, Dubai, Bangkok, Andersen AFB in Guam, Honolulu, and Acapulco.

In April 1996, an Air France Concorde was painted in Pepsi-Cola livery for an advertising campaign. This lasted for two weeks as Pepsi undertook a massive $500 million US rebranding project, which had been in the pipeline for about two years. Pepsi had been looking for something spectacular to advertise its new brand style

ABOVE: The flypast to mark the Queen's Golden Jubilee in 2002 involved 27 aircraft – including Concorde. It was the largest formation flight over London since 1981.

LEFT: Flanked by the Red Arrows, Concorde makes a flypast over the Scottish Parliament in Edinburgh after it was officially opened by the Queen.

and settled on Concorde as the ideal ambassador – even though the most commonly served soft drink on board was its arch rival Coca-Cola.

Concorde and the Red Arrows flew together again on June 2, 1996, as part of the 50th anniversary celebrations of the opening of Heathrow Airport, which was once a small, mostly military airfield, a far cry from the international airport of today. This time it was the turn of Concorde G-BOAA to fly with the bright red Hawk jets.

By its 30th flight anniversary on March 2, 1999, Concorde had clocked up 920,000 flight hours, including more than 600,000 of them at supersonic speed. Another team-up with the Red Arrows took place in July that year for the opening of the new Scottish Parliament. G-BOAE and the display team flew together over the Firth of Forth, central Edinburgh, Loch Lomond and Glasgow to mark the official opening by Her Majesty the Queen in July 1999.

The Post Office issued a new set of stamps on May 2, 2002, celebrating 50 years since the world's first scheduled passenger jet service on the de Havilland Comet. The stamps celebrated the beginnings of the jet age in civil aviation and Royal Mail used the anniversary to acknowledge the technological advancements and achievements in British aircraft engineering – from the first jet airliner through the Airbus 340-600. One of the most popular stamps was the one featuring Concorde.

That same month a rehearsal took place for the Queen's Golden Jubilee fly-past and featured Concorde G-BOAD in a formation which also included the Red Arrows, a C-17 Globemaster III, a Tristar, four Tornados, an E-3D Sentry, a VC10, two Jaguars, a Nimrod, two Canberras, a BAe 146 and two BAe125s. The fleet formed up over the North Sea and then flew south of Norwich, Old Buckenham, Shropham, to the south of Watton, and south of Swaffham, adjacent to Cockley Cley, and directly over RAF Marham. At the Concorde controls were Captain Mike Bannister from British Airways and Captain Jock Reid from the CAA.

A few days later the Royal Family was treated to the spectacle in the skies during the finale of the Queen's Golden Jubilee weekend on June 4, 2002, when the same aircraft flew overhead minus one Red Arrows Hawk and plus one Eurofighter Typhoon.

The fly-past was watched by members of the Royal Family from the balcony of Buckingham Palace, while more than one million well-wishers packed the Mall and surrounding streets for one of the most incredible displays of pageantry London had witnessed since VE Day at the end of the Second World War.

ABOVE: A sign of the times and a special occasion for all the wrong reasons – British troops guard Heathrow on February 12, 2003, as Concorde departs for New York after a suspected terrorist threat.

LEFT: Preparations for Comic Relief Day in 1988 included Concorde donning a clown's nose at Heathrow with Tony Tobias – owner of the world's longest nose.

The fleet formed-up in separate holding patterns over the North Sea and then flew over the Suffolk coastline at Southwold just after 6pm and headed over Ipswich, Chelmsford, Fairlop Waters Country Park and north-east of Ilford, before flying into central London. At 6.25pm the massive fly-past flew straight down the Mall then over Buckingham Palace at a height of 1500ft and at a speed of 280 knots.

Concorde was caught up in a terror threat on February 12, 2003. The intelligence services had warned that Heathrow was likely to be targeted by militants linked to al-Qaida who, it was feared, were armed with anti-aircraft missiles. Around 1000 police and 450 soldiers from the 1st Battalion of the Grenadier Guards and the Household Cavalry mounted in Scimitar armoured vehicles were sent to guard the airport. The conducted patrols along Heathrow's long perimeter fence and nearby open spaces, including Windsor Great Park. In the midst of the military clampdown, Concorde services continued.

There was one final record to be broken even when Concorde was retired. On its way to Seattle's Museum of Flight in November 2003, G-BOAG set a New York to Seattle speed record of three hours 55 minutes 12 seconds.

"THE FLY-PAST WAS WATCHED BY MEMBERS OF THE ROYAL FAMILY FROM THE BALCONY OF BUCKINGHAM PALACE, WHILE MORE THAN ONE MILLION WELL-WISHERS PACKED THE MALL AND SURROUNDING STREETS FOR ONE OF THE MOST INCREDIBLE DISPLAYS OF PAGEANTRY LONDON HAD WITNESSED SINCE VE DAY AT THE END OF THE SECOND WORLD WAR."

Hello, I must be going

Concorde's role in Live Aid

When Bob Geldof and Midge Ure wrote and produced the charity single Do They Know It's Christmas? in 1984 they had no idea how successful it would be – raising £8 million for famine relief. Once the cash started flooding in and musicians who'd not been featured on the single began to offer their help for any future efforts, Geldof set his sights on a more ambitious venture that would, in part, involve Concorde's extraordinary turn of speed.

The Live Aid concert at Wembley Arena in 1985 has become a musical and cultural landmark. Everyone who was anyone from the world of pop music at the time signed up to perform – Queen, David Bowie, Elton John, The Who, Dire Straits, U2, Paul McCartney, Sting and... Phil Collins.

Taking part in the London event though, meant it would be impossible to also participate in the second Live Aid event being run in parallel in Philadelphia's JFK Stadium.

There was a choice to be made and while some Brits opted for the London show, many more such as the surviving members of Led Zeppelin, Eric Clapton, the Rolling Stones and Duran Duran decided to play America instead.

At the time, Collins was riding high on the success of his third solo album No Jacket Required which reached number one in charts all over the world and spawned hit singles such as Sussudio and One More Night. The LP had appeared in January and six months of touring followed, starting in February, with Collins' regular crew of backup musicians nicknamed The Hot Tub Club.

Collins, who had already appeared on the Band Aid single playing drums, had heard about the Live Aid concert from Sting. When he saw that it was scheduled for July he realised that not only was it a great opportunity to raise some money for a good cause, it would also make the perfect climax for his 88 date world tour – which ended with a two-night stand at New York on July 1-2, having already included a show in Philadelphia on May 20.

Having made the decision to play, he then struggled to decide which show he should play.

He later recalled: "When we looked at who was on in England, there was really

nobody that I might have wanted to play with or that I knew or that I thought would want to have me.

"It needed to be someone with whom I would gel because I wanted it to be right for the concert and make a proper contribution. All my mates like Clapton and Robert Plant were doing the American show.

"Then someone said to me that it would be possible to do both if I went on early enough in London and then got Concorde. So I said: 'okay, I'll do that then', without really thinking about it. A week before Live Aid, my tour had finished in New York and while I was there, I said to this guy at the airport: 'We're coming through next week to do a charity show; any chance of getting cleared on board'? He said no. Apparently everyone has to go through the terminal – even Princess Margaret."

The London leg of Live Aid kicked off at noon with the Coldstream Guards playing a short royal salute and God Save the Queen before Status Quo took to the stage for a rousing rattle through Rockin' All Over The World, Caroline and Don't Waste My Time. They were followed by Paul Weller in The Style Council, The Boomtown Rats, Adam Ant, Ultravox, Spandau Ballet, Elvis Costello, Nik Kershaw and Sade. Then, at 3.18pm, it was Collins' turn.

After an introduction by Noel Edmonds, he joined Sting and jazz performer Branford Marsalis for a seven song set lasting 32 minutes. The capacity audience at Wembley was treated to Roxanne, Driven To Tears, Against All Odds (Take A Look At Me Now), Message In A Bottle, In The Air Tonight, Long Long Way To Go and Every Breath You Take. It was now 3.50pm, which meant that it was 10.50am in Philadelphia and Collins had eight hours and 50 minutes to get from the stage at Wembley to the stage at JFK Stadium in time to perform with Eric Clapton at 7.40pm.

ABOVE: Prince Charles and Princess Diana watch Live Aid. Seated behind are Brian May, left, and Roger Taylor, right, of Queen who would perform later that day.

BELOW: After a quick change of outfit, Phil Collins prepares to jump into a car for the short journey to Noel Edmonds' helicopter and his onward journey to Philadelphia via Concorde.

CHAPTER TWELVE

The capacity crowd at Wembley Stadium during the British leg of Live Aid.

Who played what at Live Aid – Part 1

Wembley Stadium, London (local times)

12 noon Coldstream Guards – Royal Salute, God Save the Queen.

12.02pm Status Quo – Rockin' All Over the World, Caroline, Don't Waste My Time.

12.19pm The Style Council – You're the Best Thing, Big Boss Groove, Internationalists, Walls Come Tumbling Down.

12.44pm The Boomtown Rats – I Don't Like Mondays, Drag Me Down, Rat Trap, For He's a Jolly Good Fellow (sung by the audience).

1pm Adam Ant – Vive Le Rock.

1.16pm Ultravox – Reap the Wild Wind, Dancing With Tears in My Eyes, One Small Day, Vienna.

1.47pm Spandau Ballet – Only When You Leave, Virgin, True.

2.07pm Elvis Costello – All You Need Is Love.

2.22pm Nik Kershaw – Wide Boy, Don Quixote, The Riddle, Wouldn't It Be Good.

2.55pm Sade – Why Can't We Live Together, Your Love Is King, Is It a Crime.

3.18pm Sting and Phil Collins – Roxanne, Driven to Tears, Against All Odds (Take a Look at Me Now), Message in a Bottle, In the Air Tonight, Long Long Way to Go, Every Breath You Take.

3.50pm Howard Jones – Hide and Seek.

4.07pm Bryan Ferry (with Pink Floyd's David Gilmour on guitar) – Sensation, Boys And Girls, Slave to Love, Jealous Guy.

4.38pm Paul Young – Do They Know It's Christmas? (intro), Come Back and Stay, That's the Way Love Is (with Alison Moyet), Every Time You Go Away.

5.20pm U2 – Sunday Bloody Sunday, Bad (with snippets of Satellite of Love), Ruby Tuesday, Sympathy for the Devil and Walk on the Wild Side.

6pm Dire Straits – Money for Nothing (with Sting), Sultans of Swing.

6.44pm Queen – Bohemian Rhapsody/Radio Ga Ga, Hammer to Fall, Crazy Little Thing Called Love, We Will Rock You/We Are the Champions.

ABOVE: Still feeling fresh before his flight to the US by Concorde is Phil Collins, left, with Sting on stage during the Live Aid concert at London's Wembley Stadium, England, July 13, 1985.

7.22pm David Bowie (with Thomas Dolby on keyboards) – TVC 15, Rebel Rebel, Modern Love, Heroes.

8pm The Who – My Generation/Pinball Wizard, Love, Reign o'er Me, Won't Get Fooled Again.

8.50pm Elton John – I'm Still Standing, Bennie and the Jets, Rocket Man, Don't Go Breaking My Heart (with Kiki Dee), Don't Let the Sun Go Down on Me (with George Michael and backing vocals by Andrew Ridgeley), Can I Get a Witness.

9.48pm Freddie Mercury and Brian May (Queen) – Is This the World We Created?

9.51pm Paul McCartney – Let It Be (joined by Bob Geldof, David Bowie, Pete Townshend and Alison Moyet on backing vocals).

9.54pm Band Aid (led by Bob Geldof) – Do They Know It's Christmas?

Fans jam Philadelphia's JFK Stadium during the Live Aid concert.

Edmonds, a licensed pilot, flew Collins to Heathrow airport in his own helicopter. Collins later said: "When we got to the airport – I'll never forget this – we landed and all the baggage handlers were out by Concorde to wave me goodbye. It was ever so nice of them. Cher was on the plane and I'd never met her before so I went over and said hello – you know, 'Hi, I bought I Got You Babe' – and she asked what was going on. I told her about Live Aid and she asked whether I could get her on. I told her to just turn up.

"I was supposed to do a live broadcast from Concorde. The captain obviously knew about it and said I could do it but that I wasn't to tell anybody because he wasn't supposed to let me. I thought this was crazy. Here he was telling me not to tell anybody and the broadcast's about to go out to 1.5 billion people."

Concorde touched down at New York's JFK airport after around three and a half hours in the air but with the clock ticking, Collins knew he had to get a move on. Fortunately, there was another helicopter waiting for him in anticipation of the onward journey to Philadelphia.

"Considering the distance is only a hundred and fifty miles it seemed like ages after it took us only a few hours to go all the way from London to New York," he said. "I was worried that we weren't going to arrive in time to play with the people I was supposed to play with."

When he arrived, Collins had to quickly prepare himself for the three shows he was scheduled to perform. He'd had no time to rehearse with either Eric Clapton or Led Zeppelin, whose Robert Plant, Jimmy Page and John Paul Jones were playing together again for the first time since the death of drummer John Bonham five years earlier.

With Clapton, he played an old Cream favourite, White Room, then She's Waiting and finally Derek & The Dominos crowd pleaser Layla. After only a short rest and a reintroduction by Bette Midler and Jack Nicholson, he was back for a short solo set consisting of Against All Odds (Take A Look At Me Now) and In The Air Tonight. Then, finally, he was back for the third time in a row with Plant, Page, Jones, second drummer Tony Thompson from The Power Station and bass player Paul Martinez from Plant's Band of Joy.

The performance should have been a triumphant conclusion to an heroic endeavour, only made possible by Concorde's own incredible supersonic performance but a lack of planning at the American end proved decisive.

The impromptu group's three song show turned into a shambles. First up was Rock and Roll, followed by Whole Lotta Love and Stairway to Heaven. From the outset, it was clear that the lack of opportunity to rehearse was going to be a serious problem. Neither Collins nor Thompson was able to recreate John Bonham's complex rhythms and intricate fills and it showed. To make matters worse, Page found that his guitar was out of tune and given the tight schedule, with Crosby, Stills, Nash & Young waiting in the wings to go on, there was little time to sort it out.

Collins later remarked that he had been made to feel uncomfortable by Page who, he said, was performing below his best. He told Spin magazine in 2010: "If I could have walked off, I would have – but then we'd be talking about why Phil Collins walked off from Led Zeppelin. So I just stayed there and bit my tongue."

Page himself told the BBC: "We came together and rehearsed with a drummer we'd never met before and then we were joined by Phil Collins, who we'd never played with before, on this great Live Aid stage. We went there with the spirit of it, but actually it was pretty shambolic."

Having given one performance at 3.18pm, and then three more at effectively 12.40am, the last of which was a nerve jangling disaster, Collins found that he was utterly spent.

He said: "Before I had done all this running around I was asked to sing a couple of lines in We Are The World at the end of the show and at the time I had said: 'Yeah, no problem'. But when I came off, it was like someone had unplugged me; I was completely zonked."

Collins flew back to London the day after the concert with his second wife Jill.

"It was really the next morning, when we woke up and read all the newspapers, that we actually realised what we had been part of. At the time, as far as I was concerned, it was just a logistical exercise, getting from A to B. Would I get there in time? Would it be all right? Would I lose my voice? People are still asking me if I've recovered from it; that I must have had jetlag. But we didn't, because we weren't there long enough to adjust."

Robert Plant and Jimmy Page during their hair-raising performance on July 13. On drums were both Phil Collins and Tony Thompson.

Eric Clapton performs during the American Live Aid show – Phil Collins was providing the percussion.

Who played what at Live Aid – Part 2

JFK Stadium, Philadelphia (local times)

8.51am Bernard Watson – All I Really Want to Do, Interview.
9.02am Joan Baez – Amazing Grace/We Are the World.
9.12am The Hooters – And We Danced, All You Zombies.
9.33am Four Tops – Shake Me, Wake Me (When It's Over), Bernadette, It's the Same Old Song, Reach Out I'll Be There, I Can't Help Myself (Sugar Pie, Honey Bunch).
9.45am Billy Ocean – Caribbean Queen, Loverboy.
9.52am Black Sabbath – Children of the Grave, Iron Man, Paranoid.
10.12am Run D.M.C. – Jam Master Jay, King Of Rock.
10.30am Rick Springfield – Love Somebody, State of the Heart, Human Touch.
10.47am REO Speedwagon – Can't Fight This Feeling, Roll With the Changes.
11.15pm Crosby, Stills and Nash – Southern Cross, Teach Your Children, Suite: Judy Blue Eyes.
11.26pm Judas Priest – Living After Midnight, The Green Manalishi (With The Two-Pronged Crown), You've Got Another Thing Comin'.
12.02pm Bryan Adams – Kids Wanna Rock, Summer of '69, Tears Are Not Enough, Cuts Like a Knife.
12.40pm The Beach Boys – California Girls, Help Me, Rhonda, Wouldn't It Be Nice, Good Vibrations, Surfin' USA.
1.26pm George Thorogood and the Destroyers – Who Do You Love (with Bo Diddley), The Sky Is Crying, Madison Blues (with Albert Collins).
2.07pm Simple Minds – Ghost Dancing, Don't You (Forget About Me), Promised You a Miracle.
2.41pm The Pretenders – Time the Avenger, Message of Love, Stop Your Sobbing, Back on the Chain Gang, Middle of the Road.
3.21pm Santana and Pat Metheny – Brotherhood, Primera Invasion, Open Invitation, By the Pool/Right Now.
3.57pm Ashford & Simpson – Solid, Reach Out and Touch (Somebody's Hand) (with Teddy Pendergrass).
4.27pm Madonna – Holiday, Into the Groove, Love Makes The World Go Round.
5.14pm Tom Petty and the Heartbreakers – American Girl, The Waiting, Rebels, Refugee.
5.30pm Kenny Loggins – Footloose.
5.49pm The Cars – You Might Think, Drive, Just What I Needed, Heartbeat City.
6.07pm Neil Young – Sugar Mountain, The Needle and the Damage Done, Helpless, Nothing Is Perfect (In God's Perfect Plan), Powderfinger.
6.43pm The Power Station – Murderess, Get It On.
7.21pm Thompson Twins – Hold Me Now, Revolution (with Madonna, Steve Stevens and Nile Rodgers).
7.39pm Eric Clapton (with Phil Collins) – White Room, She's Waiting, Layla.
8.04pm Phil Collins – Against All Odds (Take a Look at Me Now), In the Air Tonight.
8.10pm Led Zeppelin Reunion – (with Jimmy Page, Robert Plant, John Paul Jones, Tony Thompson, Paul Martinez, and Phil Collins) – Rock and Roll, Whole Lotta Love, Stairway To Heaven.
8.40pm Crosby, Stills, Nash & Young – Only Love Can Break Your Heart, Daylight Again/Find The Cost of Freedom.
8.45pm Duran Duran – A View to a Kill, Union of the Snake, Save a Prayer, The Reflex.
9.20pm Patti LaBelle – New Attitude, Imagine, Forever Young, Stir It Up, Over the Rainbow, Why Can't I Get It Over.
9.50pm Hall & Oates – Out of Touch, Maneater, Get Ready (with Eddie Kendricks), Ain't Too Proud to Beg (with David Ruffin), The Way You Do the Things You Do, My Girl (with Eddie Kendricks and David Ruffin).
10.15pm Mick Jagger (with Hall & Oates/Eddie Kendricks/David Ruffin) – Lonely At the Top, Just Another Night, Miss You, State Of Shock/It's Only Rock 'n Roll (But I Like It) (reprise) (with Tina Turner).
10.39pm Bob Dylan, Keith Richards and Ronnie Wood – Ballad of Hollis Brown, When the Ship Comes In, Blowin' in the Wind.
10.55pm USA for Africa (led by Lionel Richie) – We Are the World.

ABOVE: Warren Beatty and Diane Keaton at Heathrow Airport when they left by Concorde for New York on April 3, 1979.

RIGHT: Actress Elizabeth Taylor with her daughter Liza Todd at Heathrow on Friday, July 13, 1979.

BELOW: Former Beatles star Paul McCartney with his wife Linda and Heather, 17 (left), two-year-old James, Stella, eight (centre), and Mary, 10, prepare to board Concorde at Heathrow Airport on January 12, 1980.

CHAPTER THIRTEEN

Rich, famous and supersonic

Concorde's high-flying passengers

Anyone with enough money to buy a ticket could fly by Concorde and the passenger manifest frequently included millionnaires, celebrities and political figures. It attracted those for whom luxury was a way of life as well as those who saw it as a once in a lifetime experience. Certainly, the list of those who flew Concorde during its 27 years in service reads like a who's-who of the rich and famous.

The earliest years of Concorde were not a period of wealth and excess. When commercial flights began in January 1976, Harold Wilson was Prime Minister and Britain was facing an economic crisis – inflation and unemployment were both soaring while industrial output was sluggish. Later in the year, his successor James Callaghan had to go cap in hand to the International Monetary Fund to ask for a £2.3 billion bailout.

Matters did not improve much over the next few years either. The Winter of Discontent, in 1978-9, saw mass strikes and economic turmoil which did little to encourage even the wealthiest to part with the cost of a ticket on Concorde but better times were now just around the corner. Starting in 1979, the trickle of stars using Concorde rapidly became a flood.

One of the first big names to go supersonic was actor Warren Beatty. He travelled from London to New York on April 3, 1979, with his then-girlfriend Diane Keaton. Beatty was at the peak of his powers and just six days later he was at the Dorothy Chandler Pavilion in Los Angeles for the 51st

Academy Awards. His latest film Heaven Can Wait, which he wrote, directed and starred in, was nominated for nine Oscars – best picture, best director, best actor, best supporting actor, best supporting actress, best adapted screenplay, best original score, best art direction and best cinematography. It won just one – best art direction.

Three months later on July 13, actress Elizabeth Taylor and her daughter Liza Todd, from her marriage to third husband Mike Todd, flew in from Washington on Concorde for the funeral of her second husband – actor Michael Wilding – who had died in hospital at Chichester aged 66. She'd married him as a 20-year-old starlet and they were divorced five years later. By this time Taylor was married to her sixth and penultimate husband John Warner, a politician and Second World War veteran.

Faye Dunaway, who'd starred opposite Beatty in 1967's Bonnie and Clyde, flew from London to New York on Concorde on September 17, 1979. Aged 38, she was a seasoned film veteran and between the launches of 1979's The Champ and 1980's The First Deadly Sin, neither of which particularly set the box office alight.

Having married his second wife Olivia just over a year earlier, George Harrison was also between projects when he flew to New York on board Concorde to see friends on October 20, 1979. His seventh and most recent album, the eponymously titled George Harrison, had been released on February 23 and recording of his next, Somewhere in England, was due to begin on October 30, although it would not be released until June 5, 1981, after record company executives rejected a number of the songs on it and forced Harrison to change the cover art. George Harrison the album had been preceded by a single, Blow Away, which struggled up the charts to peak at number 51. The LP itself was equally lacking in success, managing only to reach number 39 in the UK chart although it went gold in America and got to number 14.

Another former Beatle, Paul McCartney and his wife Linda took their family on Concorde in January 1980. It was just two weeks after the final live date of his last tour with Wings. In contrast to Harrison, McCartney's music was as popular as ever. His second solo album, McCartney II, was in the bag, having been recorded the previous summer, and was due for release in May of that year. It was his first solo effort since the formation of Wings in 1971 and in spite of mixed reviews from critics and a distinct lack of catchy singles, it still successfully stormed the charts on both sides of the Atlantic, reaching number one in the UK and number three in the US. Wings would last just one more year before McCartney called it a day.

Wings may have been almost over but The Police were just getting started. Sting,

LEFT: American Actress Faye Dunaway is in a hurry as she leaves London's Heathrow Airport for New York by Concorde on September 17, 1979.

ABOVE: All set to fly Concorde from Heathrow airport on January 19, 1980, are The Police. Pictured from left are Andy Summers, Sting and Stewart Copeland. They were embarking on the next leg of a mammoth nine month world tour.

RIGHT: Beatle George Harrison and his Mexican wife Olivia at Heathrow Airport when they boarded a Concorde flight for New York to visit friends on October 20, 1979.

Andy Summers and Stewart Copeland set off from Heathrow on Concorde just a few days after McCartney had passed through on their way to continue a world tour in the US. Their most recent single, Walking On The Moon, had topped the charts following its release in November 1979. The single before that, Message in a Bottle, had been their first number one. The album that spawned them both, Reggatta de Blanc, had been similarly successful before being kicked off the top spot by Fleetwood Mac's Tusk. After flying to New York, the band took a connecting flight to take them on their way to their next concert in Buffalo, Texas, on January 20.

Rod Stewart and his wife Alana Hamilton, with their 10 month old baby Kimberly, flew Concorde on June 14, 1980. Less than three years later, Stewart began an affair with his second-wife-to-be model Kelly Emberg. Musically it had been more than a year since his last album, 1978's highly successful Blondes Have More Fun, and it would be another 10 months before the release of his next album, the somewhat less well received Foolish Behaviour.

Former world heavyweight champion Floyd Patterson travelled to New York on November 19, 1980, having been in Wales for a charity show on behalf of fellow boxer Johnny Owen who died aged just 24 after a world title fight in Los Angeles. His opponent had been Mexican champion Lupe Pintor, who was substantially larger and more powerful in stature. Owen managed to hold his own until the ninth round when he was knocked to the canvas – the first time this had happened in his 28 match career. He climbed back to his feet but it was obvious that he was struggling. With a full 25 seconds of the 12th round still to go, Pintor struck him with a strong blow to the right side of his head and he went down. He didn't get back up and lay on the canvas for five minutes before being taken out of the ring. Owen underwent surgery but he never regained consciousness and fell into a coma before dying on November 4.

Actor Peter O'Toole flew by Concorde in January 1982. It was 10 months ahead of his next film, My Favorite Year, which did only modest business at the box office despite his being nominated for an Academy Award for best actor. The following year O'Toole provided the voiceover for three animated adaptations of Sherlock Holmes stories.

Another pop icon caused a stir when he prepared to fly Concorde on August 29 that year. Boy George had to be given a police escort to the aircraft after spending 20 minutes hiding from his fans. He then tried to get through a side door and told journalists to stop harassing him. A security official at the airport later described

> STING, ANDY SUMMERS AND STEWART COPELAND SET OFF FROM HEATHROW ON CONCORDE JUST A FEW DAYS AFTER McCARTNEY HAD PASSED THROUGH ON THEIR WAY TO CONTINUE A WORLD TOUR IN THE US.

ABOVE: Rod Stewart, his wife Alana Hamilton, and baby Kimberly aged 10 months at London's Heathrow Airport when they were joining a Concorde flight for New York. June 14, 1980.

RIGHT: Former world heavyweight champion Floyd Patterson leaving Heathrow Airport by Concorde for New York on Nov. 19, 1980. He had been in Wales for a charity show on behalf of the late Johnny Owen who died after a world title fight in Los Angeles.

George's actions as 'sulking'. It had been nearly a year since his band Culture Club soared to international fame with their single Do You Really Want To Hurt Me? Since then the follow-up single Time (Clock of the Heart) had failed to ignite the same level of fervor among the music loving public but the band was still riding high and their next album, Colour by Numbers, released in October 1983, was their most successful.

The British and European Ryder Cup golf team posed in front of Concorde ahead of their departure for the US on October 10, 1983. While they lost the tournament at the PGA National Golf Club in Palm Beach Gardens by one point, they demonstrated to the Americans that they were rapidly reaching a level where they would be able to win. It was the first of four occasions that Tony Jacklin was the European captain and the sole occasion that his side was defeated.

The following year it was the turn of Dudley Moore, Elton John and Mick Jagger to enter the spotlight as photographers snapped them preparing to go supersonic. Moore, due to fly on February 6, was at the peak of his film making career. During 1983, he'd played the comic lead in Lovesick and Romantic Comedy. Now he was starring in Unfaithfully Yours – which opened at the box office on February 10 – Micki & Maud and Best Defense. The first of this comedy trio saw him playing a musical composer with a murderous rage, in the second he was an overworked television reporter who has

an affair and in the third he played opposite Eddie Murphy as an engineer working on a new targeting system for an American tank.

Elton John, meanwhile, had recently married his sound engineer Renate Blauel. He'd proposed to her in a restaurant just four days before their wedding on St Valentine's Day, 1984, in Sydney, Australia. The marriage lasted three years at which point John said he could no longer deny his sexual orientation. Nevertheless, by the time he flew on Concorde on August 13, 1984, he and his wife had celebrated the success of the album they had worked on together – Breaking Hearts.

The next day, Rolling Stones singer Mick Jagger came strolling into the departure lounge. His band had released the hit Undercover LP the previous year but there had been no tour to support it and there was now a growing split between the singer and guitarist Keith Richards. Richards felt aggrieved that Jagger had signed a deal to record a solo album for CBS records when in his view he should have been concentrating on the Stones. Jagger did indeed spend much of 1984 writing material for She's The Boss and when the finished article came out in February 1985 it met with moderate success.

Photographers at Heathrow Airport took a rare snap of reclusive film star Marlon Brando passing through on October 1, 1984, bound for New York by Concorde. Having retired from the movie business in 1980

after the failure of mystery film The Formula, for which he earned a Golden Raspberry nomination for worst supporting actor, he was seldom seen in public. He returned to film-making in A Dry White Season in 1989 when he was nominated for an Academy Award for best supporting actor in his role as a human rights lawyer.

Another veteran movie star, Clint Eastwood, spoke briefly to reporters as he prepared to board Concorde on January 15, 1985. He was in the process of adding the finishing touches to Pale Rider, his first western for 10 years, and said: "I was very pleased to do it. It's good to get back in the saddle again." Pale Rider was a massive success, with Eastwood's mysterious character, Preacher, drawing parallels with the Man With No Name from 1973's High Plains Drifter. The film's title was taken from a Bible verse with reference to the fourth of God's avenging angels of the apocalypse: "And I looked, and beheld a pale horse: and his name that sat on him was Death, and Hell followed with him."

Two of the Eighties biggest music stars, Michael Jackson and Madonna, also enjoyed taking to the skies on Concorde. Jackson flew on numerous occasions and was pictured at Heathrow on April 1, 1985, with his manager Frank DiLeo. It was less than a month after the release of a single he'd written with Lionel Richie – We Are The World. Clocking in at just shy of six and a half minutes in length, the record enjoyed

MAIN IMAGE: Actor Peter O'Toole at Heathrow prior to flying to New York by Concorde on January 11, 1982.

ABOVE: Pop singer Boy George at Heathrow airport, London on August 29, 1983, before flying Concorde to New York.

sales in excess of 20 million copies, making it the fifth best selling single of all time and one of fewer than 30 singles ever to have sold 10 million or more copies worldwide. The best selling single, incidentally, is White Christmas by Bing Crosby, which has sold a staggering 50 million copies since it was first released in 1942.

DiLeo was Jackson's manager for five years from 1984 to 1989 – therefore overseeing one of the most commercially successful periods of the singer's career – and managed him again in 2009, but was probably best known for his role as gangster Tuddy Cicero in the Martin Scorsese film Goodfellas. He parted company with Jackson on February 14, 1989, after the singer accused him of tampering with his money.

Like Boy George, Madonna needed a police escort as she made her way out of Heathrow airport having flown in on Concorde on August 13, 1987. She was most

of the way through her Who's That Girl world tour and scheduled to perform in an open air concert at Roundhay Park, Leeds, two days later. Her Who's That Girl film had opened at cinemas nationwide on August 7. It was roundly panned by the critics and was considered to be a box office flop. The tour, however, was Madonna's biggest to date and, on the back of the previous year's smash hit True Blue album, had included a date in Paris where she took to the stage in front of 130,000 fans. While she was enjoying commercial success, the singer's personal life was unhappy and her difficult marriage to bad boy actor Sean Penn ended in divorce two years later.

In 1987 the Europeans won the Ryder Cup for the first time on American soil and the celebration party went on for months, including the journey home, except for one person who missed the flight. Nick Faldo's caddie Andy Prodger didn't get on the plane. He had a bottle of champagne in his bag and

when it was being X-rayed he joked "you ought to be careful with that, it might have a bomb in it". He was led away in handcuffs as the plane took off and released a day later.

On May 2, 1989, Pope John Paul II became what one American newspaper described as "the first supersonic Pope" on Air France F-BTSC. He reportedly read a book on animal behaviour during the flight.

Having flown from Paris to New York via another Air France Concorde on July 12, 1992, Guns N' Roses lead singer Axl Rose was arrested on charges stemming from an outbreak of violence at a concert in St Louis a year earlier. This was during the very peak of the band's fame, success and excess. Use Your Illusion I and II had been released at the end of 1991 and 1992 saw singles such as their covers of Live And Let Die and Knockin' On Heaven's Door, November Rain and Yesterdays receiving round the clock airtime on MTV and Radio One. Footage from the St Louis gig on July

ABOVE: The British and European Ryder Cup golf team pose in front of Concorde ahead of their departure for the US on October 10, 1983. From the left are Ken Brown, Sandy Lyle, Gordon J Brand, captain Tony Jacklin, Bernard Gallacher, Jose-Maria Canizares, Ian Woosnam, Nick Faldo and Brian Waites.

ABOVE RIGHT: Comic actor Dudley Moore at Heathrow on February 6, 1984. He was close to the peak period of his film career.

LEFT: Elton John at Heathrow prior to flying by Concorde to New York on August 13, 1984. On February 14 that year he had married his sound engineer Renate Blauel.

RIGHT: Reclusive movie star Marlon Brando at Heathrow heading for the Concorde flight to New York on October 1, 1984.

2, 1991, actually held outside the city at the Riverport Amphitheater in Maryland Heights, Missouri, shows Rose dropping his microphone to the stage during a performance of Rocket Queen and leaping into the crowd at a fan who is recording the show with a video camera. What happens next is unclear, although a member of the stage crew quickly dives in to extract the singer. Rose then left the gig and fans rioted, causing $200,000 worth of damage.

On November 26, 1993, to raise money for the BBC charity Children in Need, Madness singer Suggs made what was considered to be the 'world's longest putt' down the aisle of Concorde's cabin. Due to the aircraft's supersonic speed, the short putt down the aisle actually carried the ball more than 1300 yards.

Unfortunately, Suggs' record didn't stand for long. Spanish golfer Jose Maria Olazabal took his own putt during a Concorde flight to the US on the eve of the 1999 Ryder Cup.

His 150ft putt, with Concorde travelling at 1270mph, meant the ball was actually in motion for 9.232 miles or 16,248 yards.

Richard Branson and presenter Chris Evans boarded Concorde for a night out on January 21, 1997. It came after the end of Evans' tenure as the host of the Radio 1. The previous year, he'd been criticised for a tasteless joke made about Holocaust victim Anne Frank and told by his friend and Radio 1 controller Matthew Bannister to tread more carefully. Evans responded by branding Bannister 'The Fat Controller'. In November it was clear that Evans was having problems as he declared live on air that he was medically unfit to be on the radio. Bannister gave him more holiday allowance but this was not enough and he simply stopped turning up for work.

The Beckhams flew Concorde both individually and as a family. Having travelled in style as a Spice Girl, Victoria Beckham knew there was no better way to fly across

the Atlantic which is why when she was having a wedding dress created in New York she flew three times on Concorde for fittings.

David Beckham, then her husband-to-be, flew Concorde in 1998 when he was part of the England World Cup squad which competed in France that summer. He later became a regular passenger.

Diana Ross also loved flying Concorde, well mostly. In September 1999, she hit the newspaper headlines when she was arrested on Concorde after she allegedly assaulted a female security officer trying to make a search before she boarded the plane. After a quick enquiry the soul star was eventually cautioned and then released.

In 2000, Robbie Williams had to be in London to personally accept two Brit Awards. He could have sent a video acceptance, but felt that it was more appropriate to be there in person and flew Concorde as a result.

ABOVE: Pop star Michael Jackson leaves Heathrow Airport to fly to New York on Concorde on April 1, 1985, after a short stay in Britain. To his right is his manager, Frank DiLeo.

RIGHT: Rolling Stones lead singer Mick Jagger at Heathrow on August 14, 1984. During this period he was working on songs for his first solo album She's The Boss.

TOP: Veteran actor Clint Eastwood was in the process of completing Pale Rider, his first western for 10 years when he flew Concorde on January 15, 1985.

ABOVE: Madonna is escorted through Heathrow by policemen after stepping off her Concorde flight on August 13, 1987.

The Police having long since disbanded, Sting was one of the first famous faces to get back on board Concorde following the air crash in Paris in 2000 and the terrorist attacks of September 11, 2001. Speaking on November 7, he hailed the relaunched aircraft as "a symbol of normal life" and said: "I would like to get back to that – some people in America are too afraid to leave their homes. They need to be encouraged to travel."

Less than a week later, film star Hugh Grant boarded the aircraft bound for New York. It was seven months after the release of the second most successful film of his career to date – Bridget Jones's Diary. This was also the second in a series of six movies starring Grant that would net a grand total of $1.2 billion. The first was 1999's Notting Hill and the remainder were Two Weeks Notice, About a Boy, Love Actually and Bridget Jones: The Edge of Reason.

His partner of 13 years Liz Hurley flew on Concorde not long afterwards on January 3, 2002. At the time she was pregnant by ex-boyfriend Steve Bing and gave birth on April 4 of that year to Damian Charles Hurley. Bing, an American businessman, film producer and heir to a $600 million fortune, had denied paternity but a DNA test established that he was indeed the boy's father.

Not every celebrity enjoyed their Concorde experience. James Bond actor Roger Moore seemed destined never to have a good relationship with the aircraft. Once, on his way to board a flight to Rio de Janeiro at Paris Charles de Gaulle Airport, to film Moonraker, he felt a sharp and sudden pain. It was a kidney stone and he was rushed first to the airport's emergency room and then to a Paris hospital. It was three days later that he finally made the trip. His disenchantment worsened after two of his friends died in the 2000 crash. He also once commented that the seats on the Concorde were cramped and the fare "was very expensive".

Irish TV chat show presenter Graham Norton also had a negative experience on March 15, 2002. He was one of the passengers on board the New York-bound aircraft when Captain Paul Douglas abandoned the take-off at Heathrow airport. A computer error caused an engine to accelerate too quickly. The plane was full of passengers flying to America for Liza Minnelli's wedding and for New York's St Patrick's Day parade. It was taken out of service and examined by BA engineers. Meanwhile, the affected passengers were able to leave on another Concorde albeit four hours late.

Halle Berry took a trip on Concorde on February 20, 2002, eight months before her

Passengers behaving badly

While most of Concorde's passengers behaved themselves impeccably and were happy to simply enjoy the fine foods they were served and be entertained by the incredible view from its windows, some sought pleasure elsewhere.

Freddie Mercury was notorious for his bad behaviour on board the aircraft, once claiming to have snorted cocaine off one of its toilet seats. His personal manager later commented: "Freddie didn't need the plane. He was so high on drugs he could have flown the Atlantic by himself."

The Queen singer is said to have once hired Concorde just to fly himself and 99 close friends to New York for a month long party. He promised his guests: "The only thing you'll have to pay for will be the condoms."

In May 2003, a pair of Spanish Concorde passengers claimed to have joined the 11 mile high club by having sex on one of the aircraft's seats while covered with a blanket. At the time, a British Airways spokesman said: "We certainly want the last few months of Concorde to be a celebration – but this pair celebrated a bit more than we expected. We only hope that the earth moved for them at twice the speed of sound."

The couple had paid £1999 each for their seats on the BA001 flight from London to New York.

LEFT: Members of Madness, the Bee Gees and Right Said Fred, with singers Kiki Dee and Gabrielle (holding the bear) are pictured shortly before takeoff aboard Concorde at Heathrow to raise money for the BBC's Children in Need appear on November 26, 1993.

ABOVE: Guns N' Roses singer Axl Rose is escorted to a police car at New York's John F Kennedy airport after being arrested as he stepped off an Air France Concorde from Paris on, July 12, 1992.

BELOW: Prime Minister Tony Blair and his wife Cherie prepare to board Concorde at Heathrow for their flight to Washington D. C. on February 4, 1998.

latest film, Die Another Day, opened at box offices around the world. She played Giacinta 'Jinx' Johnson, a National Security Agency agent, and in one scene she emerges from the ocean in an orange bikini and white belt in a homage to Ursula Andress's character Honey Ryder in the first Bond film, Dr No. The film would go on to take a staggering $432 million dollars, making it the most successful Bond film of the modern era with ticket prices adjusted for inflation.

A third former Beatle and one of the surviving two, Ringo Starr, flew Concorde with his wife Barbara on December 2, 2002. Earlier that year he had been inducted into the Percussive Arts Society Hall of Fame and just three days before his flight, on November 29, 2002, he had performed at a concert in the Royal Albert Hall to mark the first anniversary of George Harrison's death. He had played Photograph and a cover of Carl Perkins' Honey Don't at the Concert for George.

Transatlantic chat show presenter David Frost called Concorde his "time machine", since it enabled him to fly to New York to record a TV programme and return to London in time for supper. After the aircraft flew for the last time he said he had lost count of the number of times he had been a Concorde passenger, estimating a figure of between 300 and 500 trips.

Politicians loved Concorde too. James Callaghan became the first supersonic Prime Minister when he flew on Concorde to Washington D. C. to negotiate landing rights in the United States in March 1977. Former Defence Secretary Geoff Hoon's journey on the luxury jet at taxpayers' expense caused controversy when he was a junior minister. His Cabinet colleague Dr Jack Cunningham was also forced to explain himself when it was revealed that he flew Concorde to Washington at a cost of £3452 when he could have caught a business class flight just minutes earlier at a fraction of the cost.

As Prime Minister, Margaret Thatcher took her time before jumping aboard the luxury airliner. It was not until 1986 that she flew Concorde for the first time, having been in power for seven years. When she did it was to attend Expo 86 in Vancouver, US.

ABOVE: Richard Branson (left) and Chris Evans at Heathrow before boarding Concorde for a flight to New York for a night out on January 21, 1997.

RIGHT: TV presenter Graham Norton outside Channel 4 headquarters in London. On March 15, 2002, he was one of the celebrities on board a British Airways Concorde that had to abort its take off at Heathrow after an engine problem.

LEFT: Diana Ross, wearing a jumpsuit, runs through Heathrow Airport to board Concorde for the second time, after spending part of the day in custody at the airport's police station on September 22, 1999.

RIGHT: Singer Sting prepares to board Concorde not long after the 9/11 attacks. The date is November 7, 2001.

John Major followed her as Prime Minster and he also flew Concorde, taking off to Washington in 1995 for a meeting with President Clinton. The man who defeated him to become PM in his stead, Tony Blair, visited Clinton by Concorde himself in February 1998 with his wife Cherie.

Actress Joan Collins was also a great fan of Concorde and flew transatlantic many times. In a 'diary' article for The Spectator of November 1, 2003, after Concorde's final flight from New York to London, she wrote: "I was as excited as a kid going to Disneyland to be invited on Concorde's last flight from New York to London.

"I've always regarded it as one of Britain's greatest ambassadors, and we considered that being a part of its final journey was too

important a historic event to miss. Percy and I thus arrived at a darkened and seemingly deserted JFK airport at 6am for a 7am flight. Are we the first?, I inquired of the charming special services representative. 'No, you're the last,' was the reply. 'The party's been going for hours.'

"We checked in without luggage, which for me is itself a historic event, but I still managed to pocket a couple of Concorde luggage tags, which I understand are now selling for £17 on eBay along with various other mementos from the iconic aircraft, including memorabilia catalogues, safety cards and a bathroom sign. God only knows how they took that off."

She said she set off the security alarm by wearing too much "bling".

"Shortly after my return the flight was called and the entire New York BA staff lined up to say their goodbyes to everyone, many of them with a tear in their eye," she wrote. "It was still dark outside, but it seemed as though the entire airport ground staff had stopped what they were doing and stood on the Tarmac to wave and cheer. On board, the champagne was passed around lavishly as we privileged few buckled up and prepared for the last ride. I clutched my husband's hand as the brakes were released and the power of a sudden 250mph acceleration threw us against the back of our seats, like some insanely powerful hot-rod competition, and then majestically soared into the air like a beautiful and graceful prehistoric bird."

ABOVE: Actress Joan Collins waits with other passengers before the last commercial flight of the British Airways Concorde at John F Kennedy International Airport in New York on Friday, October 24, 2003.

RIGHT: Bond girl Halle Berry at Heathrow on February 20, 2002. She appeared in Die Another Day later that year.

BELOW: Manchester United manager Alex Ferguson waves to the media from the cockpit of Concorde as his team fly out to Barcelona for the European Champions' Cup final against Bayern Munich on May 26, 1999.

TOP: Riding a wave of immense popularity thanks to his roles in films such as Notting Hill and Bridget Jones's Diary, Hugh Grant readies himself to leave Heathrow Airport for New York by Concorde on November 12, 2001.

ABOVE: England midfield player David Beckham (centre) and Gary Neville arrive at Heathrow on Concorde on July 1, 1998.

Royal Concorde

Flying the monarch and her family

As the most luxurious form of transport available anywhere in the world, and a symbol of British technological prowess and innovation, Concorde was frequently called upon to carry members of the royal family on both official and unofficial visits.

Ranking among Britain's most frequent fliers, the royal family have had access to an enviable selection of air transport, both civilian and military, since 1936 in the form of first the King's Flight and later the Queen's Flight.

Even before then, royalty had been no stranger to flight with the future King Edward VIII becoming the first to learn how to pilot an aircraft while he served with British forces in France during the First World War as Prince of Wales.

The royals took a keen interest in Concorde right from the start, an interest that manifested itself in several flights in the aircraft, even though the Queen's Flight with its 'official' aircraft was always available.

The Duke of Edinburgh might have been a Royal Navy man but he has always been supportive of all the armed services and thoroughly enjoyed being involved in all their activities. As well as sailing he has always had a love of flying. Concorde was a project close to his heart, which is why he could not resist getting a closer look during a ground inspection in early January 1972.

He was not the only royal there as Prince Bernhard of the Netherlands was also interested. They were shown around by test pilot Brian Trubshaw who later became a great friend of the royal family. When Trubshaw died in 2001, among the many tributes that poured in were those from Buckingham Palace. A spokesman said: "The Duke is very sad."

Trubshaw was awarded the CBE in 1970 and was known as "my Brian" by the Queen, who knew him from his days with the King's Flight, her father's air transport corps, after the war.

As a man of action though, a 'look around' was not enough for Prince Philip, who could not wait to fly at supersonic speed. His wish came true when he joined a test flight on January 13, 1972, and later emerged beaming after the experience of Mach 2 – having taken the controls himself while the aircraft flew over the Bay of Biscay during a 92 minute flight.

He said afterwards that it had been very impressive but complained that he was difficult to tell how fast you were going at that speed: "It was very disappointing from

ABOVE: Princess Anne scribbles a message, seated beside her fiance Captain Mark Phillips, in Concorde 002, in which they were to fly supersonic on October 23, 1973.

LEFT: The Red Arrows and Concorde fly over the Queen Victoria memorial outside the front of Buckingham Palace, during the fly past by the RAF to mark the Queen's Golden Jubilee in 2002. The Queen herself was delighted to see Concorde fly.

OPPOSITE: Queen Elizabeth II and the Duke of Edinburgh step from a British Airways Concorde on arrival at Kuwait Airport on February 14, 1979.

ABOVE: Flying home from Bridgetown, Barbados, in Concorde after her silver jubilee tour of the Caribbean, the Queen looks through a photo album. The date is November 2, 1977.

RIGHT: Prince Andrew at Heathrow Airport in London with his cabin luggage before boarding a Concorde flight to New York with his detective and a valet on July 14, 1983. He was attending America's Cup victory ball at Newport, Rhode Island.

that point of view. Any complications are not apparent when you are sitting or flying in it. All the genius is in little boxes."

At the time the prince had already clocked up more than 2200 hours of flying time on 24 different types of aircraft.

Princess Margaret had a reputation as a jet-setter, and she also became a devotee of Concorde. She first flew in it in May 1972 and never concealed her love of it.

Princess Diana also flew Concorde as did virtually all the royal family who were around during its 27 years in service. When the first commercial flights by British Airways and Air France took off in synchronised fashion from Heathrow and Charles de Gaulle in 1976, there were many dignitaries on board the two planes including the Duke of Kent who was on the BA flight over the Alps to Bahrain.

He later commented that is was: "an amazing experience and a tribute to everyone who played a part in the creation of

"PRINCESS MARGARET HAD A REPUTATION AS A JET-SETTER, AND SHE ALSO BECAME A DEVOTEE OF CONCORDE."

this magnificent aeroplane. It has everything, speed, comfort and a great future".

The Queen Mother, who had once remarked to a British Airways captain that she had never flown on Concorde, finally did so on August 6, 1985, to celebrate her 85th birthday.

On Concorde's first day in commercial service, the Queen sent a message to French President Valery Giscard d'Estaing saying: "On the occasion of today's inaugural flight by Concorde aircraft of Air France and British Airways, I send you and the French people my warmest congratulations. Today's flights mark the successful outcome of 14 years of close collaboration between our two nations. It is a source of pride that our countries have today inaugurated a new era in civil aviation."

On November 2, 1977, she travelled for the first time aboard Concorde herself. The aircraft was G-BOAE and it was during the silver jubilee celebrations and Her Majesty flew from the Sir Grantley Adams International Airport, Barbados, to London Heathrow. That occasion was also the first visit by a Concorde aircraft to Barbados. The Alpha Echo aircraft in which the Queen travelled was also the last Concorde to fly supersonic to Barbados, on November 17, 2003 – a delivery flight to the Barbados Concorde Experience museum where it remains on display.

That first flight followed a cruise in the Grenadines. The Queen arrived at Bridgetown harbour on-board the Royal Yacht Britannia on the last leg of her silver

The usual royal aircraft – a Sikorsky S-76 C++ helicopter painted in the red and blue colours of the Brigade of Guards.

The Queen's (and King's) Flight

Members of the royal family are often called upon to carry out engagements across the UK and overseas and the Queen in particular has to travel to countries and places never possible for her predecessors.

While Concorde was frequently used by royals while it was in service, there were also many other aircraft types that were made available.

The Royal Travel Office at Buckingham Palace has the task not only of coordinating different types of aircraft for use by royals, but also of ensuring that their use is appropriate and cost-effective.

During visits within the UK, the official aircraft of royalty is a Sikorsky S-76 C++ helicopter painted in the

red and blue colours of the Brigade of Guards. This is operated by the Royal Household from Blackbushe Aerodrome in Hampshire.

The cost of official royal travel by air is met by the Royal Travel Grant, part of the Government's annual funding for the royal family.

Although he had flown before as the Prince of Wales, King Edward VIII became the first British monarch to fly in 1936.

A formal procedure was established for royal flights on July 21, 1936, with the creation of The King's Flight at Hendon in North London. This operated a twin-engine de Havilland Dragon Rapide, G-ADDD, which had formerly been King Edward VIII's private aircraft.

This was replaced in May 1937 by an Airspeed AS.6 Envoy III, G-AEXX. It was the first aircraft purchased specifically for The King's Flight.

The flight was disbanded during the Second World War, as royals used military aircraft instead, but was reformed in 1946. Now based at RAF Benson it boasted four Vickers Vikings. The following year all of them were used during a royal tour of South Africa.

Over the years, many royals have earned their pilot's licence including the Duke of Edinburgh, the Prince of Wales, the Duke of York as a Royal Navy helicopter pilot, the Duke of Cambridge as an RAF helicopter pilot and Prince Harry as an Army Air Corps pilot.

LEFT: The Queen Mother prepares for a ride on Concorde on August 6, 1985, in belated celebration of her 85th birthday two days earlier. Pictured on the left, from left to right are Susannah Constantine and the Queen Mother's grandchildren Lady Sarah Armstrong-Jones and Viscount Linley.

FAR LEFT: During her celebratory trip, the Queen Mother visits Concorde's cockpit.

The Duchess of York, after becoming the first woman royal to gain a private pilot's licence went on the flight deck of Concorde during her visit to Heathrow Airport on March 11, 1987, as a guest of British Airways.

LEFT: Diana, Princess of Wales holds a flower with red, white, and blue ribbons given to her upon her arrival at John F Kennedy International Airport in New York on February 1, 1989. The Princess flew by Concorde jet for a three-day visit to the city.

jubilee tour. She spent a few days meeting the people, opening Parliament and attending to other state business, and then came the Concorde journey home, piloted by Captains Norman Todd and Brian Walpole, for a record-setting supersonic flight back to London Heathrow. The Queen had never flown supersonic before and clearly enjoyed it. She certainly came back for more.

At the start of November 1982 the Queen and Prince Philip flew on Concorde together and did so again in February 1984 when they flew off on a trip to the

Middle East, which took in Jordan, Kuwait and Saudi Arabia. Arriving in Concorde certainly flew the flag in the Middle East and the trip was considered a huge success for commerce as well as international relations.

In 1989, the Queen and Prince returned to Barbados, and once again Concorde made the trip and had a huge impact, as indeed it did when the royal couple flew Concorde on a state visit to America, starting with Washington, in 1991. For all their previous objections, the Americans were out in force to welcome Concorde and her royal passengers.

Is it any wonder then that Her Majesty and her family never tired of seeing this man-made icon of the skies, which was always the star of the show whenever there was a fly-past? That spectacular fly-past of the Queen's Golden Jubilee on June 4, 2002, is possibly the best example of them all. The

" THE CHEERING CROWDS BECAME EVEN LOUDER IN TRIBUTE, BUT PERHAPS THE GREATEST ACCOLADE OF THEM ALL CAME FROM HER MAJESTY THE QUEEN WHO COULD CLEARLY BE SEEN TO MOUTH THE WORDS: "LOOK, THERE'S CONCORDE"! "

Rescuing Princess Margaret

Concorde was called upon to bring Princess Margaret back to Britain from the Caribbean in 1999 after she suffered a horrific accident while having a shower.

The princess, in accommodation on the island of Mustique, was washing her hair one morning in February while the rest of her household was having breakfast. Suddenly, they were interrupted by a servant who said the princess was inside the bathroom with the door locked and there was an unusual amount of steam coming from under it.

Without hesitation, Margaret's personal detective went to the bathroom and broke down the door. Inside, he found the princess in a state of shock and badly scalded. It was later revealed that Margaret had stood in the bath with the intention of washing her hair. The shower controls were old and complicated and when she turned the water on, instead of warm water coming out of the shower head she got boiling water coming out of the taps by her feet.

This came as such a painful shock that she was unable to move until help arrived. She had also suffered a stroke the previous year. The scalding was bad enough but Margaret also suffered from a blood circulation problem which made the injuries very slow to heal.

She tried to hide the pain she was in and pretend that nothing was wrong but in the end her lady-in-waiting Anne Glenconner had to phone the Queen at Balmoral, who then arranged for Concorde to fly out and bring her sister back home via Barbados.

Princess Margaret in October 1999, eight months after her accident.

The Queen and Prince Philip disembark in Washington during a royal visit on May 20, 1991. US National Archives

LEFT: Marching through Heathrow Airport prior to boarding Concorde for a flight to New York on September 23, 1996, is Diana, Princess of Wales. She was due to meet Presidential First Lady Hillary Clinton.

cream of Royal Air Force pilots took to the skies with 27 specially selected aircraft. They had rehearsed the flight a few days earlier, and everything was set for a breath-taking spectacular.

A million people packed the Mall and other areas around Buckingham Palace and at last the roar of aircraft could be heard in the distance. Within moments the planes came into view, flying directly towards Buckingham Palace over the Mall. The excitement mounted, everyone looked up and the TV cameras provided a window for the rest of the world.

The RAF planes were magnificent, but then came the show-stealer as they provided the outriders of the sky for the mighty Concorde. The cheering crowds became even louder in tribute, but perhaps the greatest accolade of them all came from Her Majesty the Queen who could clearly be seen to mouth the words: "Look, there's Concorde"!

Untold thousands of these ugly but delicious crustaceans were consumed on board during Concorde's decades in service. They were only occasionally seen in one piece however.

CHAPTER FIFTEEN

Cordon Concorde

Dining out above the clouds

The selection of fine foods and even finer drinks available to Concorde's passengers changed from its early days in the 1970s to its final flights in 2003. Diners could rest assured however that whenever they flew they would only ever be served the very best...

Passengers aboard Concorde ranged from millionaire business jet setters and famously fussy celebrities to ordinary travellers busting their budgets to enjoy a taste of the luxury lifestyle.

But bank balance has never been an indicator of gastronomic preference and Concorde's menu planners had to come up with a selection of meals capable of pleasing every palate.

Then there was the wine list. How do you impress passengers who may well have their own carefully chosen selection of vintage wines nestling in a climate controlled cellar back home?

British Airways' solution was simple – assemble a team of top chefs to oversee the food and take on a Master of Wine from the world renowned Institute of Masters of Wine to hand-pick the bubbly, the reds, the whites and the rest.

The menu reached its zenith during Concorde's final days with all the stops very firmly being pulled out to make the supersonic dining experience one to remember for years to come. During the flight, passengers were handed an individually dated 32cm by 15cm grey booklet with a cover bearing the embossed Concorde logo.

Inside was a brief paragraph explaining how the British Airways Culinary Council had "risen to the highest challenge, creating the ultimate in-flight menu". It went on to promise that "despite space and time constraints, the culinary council has developed superior quality menus without compromising individual culinary style. We

trust that its creations will please the eye, delight the palate and, most importantly, make your journey on the Concorde the ultimate experience".

Even a cursory glance at the British Airways menu for Concorde reveals a certain Anglo-Saxon approach to the dining experience however. Veal, guinea fowl and lobster yes, but where are the bells and whistles?

The French did the top flight food a little differently. The Air France menu included scrambled eggs, edible pansies, truffles, monkfish and macaroons, not to mention oodles of French bread and mushrooms. The late-period wine was selected by

Philippe Faure-Brac, an accomplished author and winner of the world's best 'sommelier' or wine steward title in 1992.

The menu itself changed over the years but in contrast to the staid, low key and rather plain British booklets, the French preferred a more lavish affair. Some examples from the 1970s featured pictures of balloons from the 19th century, a 1980s set had riotous colours splashed across them in abstract patterns while early 1990s boasted images of oddly decorated musical instruments. Up until September 11, 2001, silver cutlery was given to passengers but after the terrorist attacks in New York this was switched for plastic utensils.

Stewardess Heather Ellis prepares a meal on the last commercial flight of Concorde from JFK to Heathrow, on the day that the supersonic airliner retired from commercial service.

Food and refreshments were prepared and served on board the aircraft from no fewer than seven 'galley' stations, four at the front of the aircraft's fuselage and three at the rear. The first of these was located at the front not far from the cockpit and housed a double oven complete with air extraction system. Beneath these were tucked two narrow trolleys for wheeling meal trays down the single central aisle. The second compact galley included a sink, twin beverage makers, meal tray compartments, a warming compartment, fold up table, faucet and a couple of wheeled carts. Galley three was where you'd find the in-flight magazines, five more meal tray containers and coat racks while the fourth galley had yet more meal tray containers and a substantial waste storage container.

At the back of the plane, the fifth and sixth galleys had a megaphone for making announcements plus extra meal tray storage and a trolley each. Right at the very back of Concorde, near the tail, the seventh galley had four meal carts, another double oven, extra storage and another pair of beverage makers – which were apparently notoriously unreliable.

Overall, the aircraft had four ovens and up to 10 trolley carts to make sure passengers never had to go without a drink and never had to wait too long for their food.

Canapés in a bewildering variety of styles were served over the years. These ones have cheese, cucumber and tangerine on them.

Master chefs of supersonic cuisine

Among the esteemed members of the British Airways Culinary Council, the top chefs behind the menu offered aboard Concorde, were Michel Roux, Shaun Hill, Richard Corrigan, Liam Tomlin, Mark Edwards and Claudia Fleming. The Master of Wine was Jancis Robinson.

Roux led the council and probably had the greatest influence on the meals served to Concorde passengers. During a lifetime of working at the cutting edge of high class cuisine he's picked up more than 40 awards and prizes for his culinary creations. He's also picked up

accolades such as the Meilleur Ouvrier de France, an honorary OBE and the Chevalier de la Legion d'Honneur.

Hill has worked at some of London's top restaurants including The Capital Hotel in Knightsbridge and Blakes in South Kensington. He really made his name at the Merchant House restaurant in Ludlow.

Irish chef Corrigan has enjoyed a successful television career on programmes such as the Great British Food Revival and Something for the Weekend on BBC2, Full on Food on BBC1

and Market Kitchen on UKTV. Tomlin, another Irishman, joined the BA team in 2000 having carved out a successful career at Banc Restaurant in Australia. Mark Edwards is another accomplished chef and Fleming is regarded as one of America's top pastry chefs.

Wine writer and critic Robinson advises the Queen on what to put in her wine cellar. In 1984, she became the first person working outside the wine trade to become a Master of Wine and has penned numerous volumes on wine tasting and appreciation.

Team leader Michel Roux.

Top chef Shaun Hill.

TV star Richard Corrigan.

Master of Wine Jancis Robinson.

The Concorde Cellar

Champagne

Krug Brut Grande Cuvée

Alfred Gratien Cuvée Paradis

Pol Roger Cuvée Sir Winston Churchill 1986

Krug Clos du Mesnil 1986

Jacquart Cuvée Nominée de Jacquart 1988

Pommery Cuvée Louise 1989

Lanson Blanc de Blancs 1990

White Burgundy

Meursault 1er Cru Poruzot 1996
La Grande Famille des Domaines

Puligny-Montrachet 1er Cru Les
Champs Gain 1996 Labouré-Roi

Corton Charlemagne Grand Cru
1996 Labouré-Roi

Chablis Grand Cru Bougros
1997 Jean-Marc Brocard

Chassagne-Montrachet 1er Cru Les Vergers
1997 Charton et Trebuchet

Chassagne-Montrachet 1er Cru Morgeot
1998 Domaine Vincent Girardin

Meursault Les Narvaux 1999
Domaine Vincent Girardin

Claret

Château Pape-Clement 1994 Grand
Cru Classé Pessac-Léognan

Château Gruaud-Larose 1994 Grand
Cru Classé Saint Julien

Château Pichon Lalande 1994 Grand
Cru Classé Pauillac

Château Smith Haut-Lafite 1994 Grand
Cru Classé Pessac-Léognan

Château La Lagune 1995 Grand
Cru Classé Medoc

Château Branaire Ducru 1995 Grand
Cru Classé Saint Julien

Château de Fieuzal 1996 Grand
Cru Classé Pessac-Léognan

Red Burgundy

Volnay 1er Cru Les Chevrets 1990 Domaine
Jean-Mac Boillot

Corton-Pougets Grand Cru 1994
Château de Corton-André

Le Corton Grand Cru 1996 La Grande
Famille des Domaines

Pommard 1er Cru Les Chanlins 1997
Domaine Vincent Girardin

Port

Warre's 1982 Colheita Port

Bar Service:

Aperitifs

Tanqueray No. Ten Gin

Smirnoff Black Label Vodka

Bacardi Carta Blanca Rum

Martini Sweet and Dry Vermouth

Tio Pepe Fino Sherry

La Concha Amontillado Sherry

Campari Bitters

Canadian Club Rye Whisky

Glenfiddich Ancient 18-Year-Old Single Malt Whisky

Johnny Walker Blue Label Whisky

Woodford Reserve

Kentucky Straight Bourbon Whisky

Cocktails

Prepared to your choice from the range
of beverages carried on board.

Soft Drinks

A selection of traditional and modern soft drinks.

Fresh orange juice,

tomato juice,

apple juice,

Highland Spring Still or

sparking mineral water,

Schweppes – Tonic,

Bitter Lemon,

Soda Water,

Malvern Mineral Water,

Coca-Cola, Diet Coke,

Canada Dry Ginger Ale,

Sprite

Beers

Lager – Grolsch,

Stella Artois, Holsten Pils,

Fuller's London Pride Ale

Digestifs & Liqueurs

The Concorde Selection

Martell XO Cognac,

Drambuie, Cointreau,

Grand Marnier,

Tia Maria, Baileys,

Amaretto di Saronno

Air France
Brunch a la carte

Wines

Champagne Cuvee Speciale
Krug Grande Cuvee

Bordeaux Blanc Liquoreux
Sauternes 1er Cru Classe 1995
Chateau Suduiraut

Bourgogne Blanc
Chablis 1er Cru 'Beauroy' 1999

Bourgogne Rouge
Volnay 1er Cru 'Les Taillepieds' 1996

Bordeaux Rouge
Saint-Emilion Grand Cru Classe 1997

Bread and pastries

Mini baguette, Walnut bread,
Cranberry bread, French bakery selection,
Preserves, honey, yoghurt.

Non-alcoholic drinks

Coffee, decaffeinated coffee,
choice of teas, herbal teas, hot chocolate.
freshly squeezed fruit juice.

Appetiser

Papaya garnished with red berries.

Choice of hot or cold dishes

Chef's special – scrambled eggs with
creamed morel mushroom fricassee
and Maine lobster.

Vegetarian hotpot –
tender mixed vegetables with truffles,
sauteed wild mushrooms,
fennel and truffle emulsion
with balsamic vinegar.

Gourmet platter – layered foie gras
and truffles, pears with Bordeaux wine,
fresh salad with a pansy* garnish.
*Edible flower.

Seafood platter – sauteed prawn
and monkfish chanterelle mushroom galette
wrapped in grilled zucchini and served
with mache and lettuce.

Selection of French regional cheeses.

Sweets

Petits fours – chocolate macaroon, pineapple fondant,
raspberry and blackcurrant tarlet.

At the end of your supersonic flight our cabin crew
will be pleased to serve you caviar with a glass of
Cuvee Speciale champagne to welcome you to Paris.

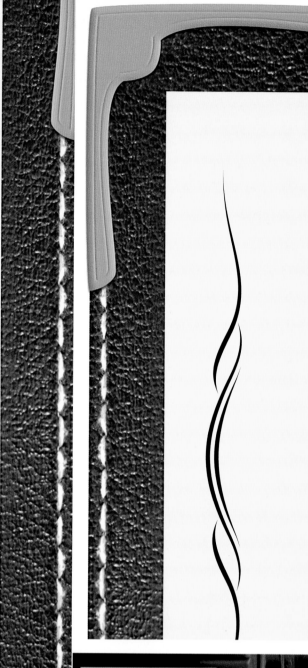

The prawn appetiser with caviar tin. Nathan Roemer

British Airways

Dinner

Canapés

Appetiser
Fresh prawn niçoise.

Entrées
Roast guinea fowl and truffle stuffing, with cep reduction and fondant potato.

Lobster fish cakes with a light shellfish sauce.

Grilled fillet of veal, black pepper and lemon butter, sauté mushroom mix, roasted sea salt potatoes.

Grilled artichoke, plum tomatoes, buffalo mozzarella on mixed leaves with balsamic dressing.

Dessert
Chocolate silk on a nut brittle base with chocolate sauce.

Or cheese.
Old Pequlier, Melusine goat's cheese, unpasteurised Dunsyre Blue.

Selection of bread rolls.

Coffee, decaffeinated coffee, a selection of tea with chocolates.

As an alternative to the full menu, we are pleased to offer a selection of freshly made sandwiches including smoked salmon and cucumber on wholemeal bread, shaved pastrami and American mustard on wholemeal bread, chicken salad on malted bread.

Brunch

Appetiser
Ballontine of salmon with crème fraîche.

Entrées
English breakfast featuring back bacon, scrambled eggs, pork sausage, tomato and mushrooms.

Lamb fillet with mustard and herb crust, spinach and sea salt roasted new potatoes.

Grilled sea bass with caviar cream sauce, Swiss chard and wild rice.

Oriental style vegetable and noodle salad with chilli and ginger dressing.

Dessert
Banana tart.

Or cheese.
Stilton, Chevre and Pont L'Eveque.

Selection of bread rolls.

Coffee, decaffeinated coffee, a selection of tea with chocolates.

As an alternative to the full menu, we are pleased to offer a selection of freshly made sandwiches including ham and cheese, egg and bacon, rocket with goats cheese.

The guinea fowl dinner selection. Nathan Roemer

Chocolate silk with coffee and chocolates. Nathan Roemer

Getting the party started: Champagne, canapés, and sparking mineral water. Nathan Roemer

Air France's Concorde flight 4590 attempts to take off from Paris Charles de Gaulle airport with fire trailing from its left wing on July 25, 2000.

When it all went wrong

The disaster that spelled the end for Concorde

During its first 24 years in service Concorde had its share of mishaps and mechanical failures, particularly burst tyres, but thousands of hours passed without incident until July 25, 2000, when a catastrophic accident resulted in the deaths of 113 people. But was Concorde at fault?

There was nothing remarkable about Flight AFR 4590 bound for New York from Paris Charles de Gaulle Airport. Tuesday, July 25, was a mild day at around 19°C, wind speed was low and it was business as usual for Air France Concorde F-BTSC and its nine-strong crew. The aircraft was topped up to its maximum fuel capacity, 94.8 tonnes, loaded up with a full complement of 100 passengers – 96 Germans, two Danes, an American and an Austrian – and their luggage, 122 items, was secured before the crew radioed air traffic control with their intention to take off at 2.30pm.

Pilot Christian Marty, 54, co-pilot Jean Marcot, 50, and flight engineer Gilles Jardinaud, 58, were making their final checks when the air traffic controller radioed at 2.07pm and gave them start-up clearance, confirming that runway 26 was cleared and ready for them. F-BTSC taxiied forward on to the runway at 2.34pm via the airport's Romeo taxiway. Final clearance for takeoff was given at 2.42pm and 14 seconds later the aircraft was on its way.

Twenty-three seconds later F-BTSC was travelling at 115mph. Concorde has eight wheels on its rear landing gear, two sets of four, and at this point the front right tyre on the left hand set suffered a jagged 32cm cut from debris lying on the runway. Large pieces of shredded rubber were thrown against the underside of the left wing and several bits

punctured one of the aircraft's 13 fuel tanks – tank five. This was not an entirely unusual occurrence – crash investigators revealed later that there had previously been 57 occasions when Concorde had suffered burst or punctured tyres. And on six of these occasions pieces of rubber had ruptured a fuel tank causing leaks.

This time it was different. Either a damaged electrical harness in the landing gear or contact with hot engine parts caused jet fuel spilling from the leak to catch fire. The flames rapidly spread under the left wing and engines one and two began to lose thrust, engine two severely so as bits of burned fuel tank and fuselage entered it. At 2.43pm and 13 seconds, the air traffic controller radioed the crew to tell them that flames could be seen under the aircraft – a situation of which they had not previously been aware. Flight engineer Jardinaud announced the failure of engine two and then Marty told him to both shut it down and activate the engine fire extinguisher.

F-BTSC was now travelling at 230mph. At 2.43pm and 59 seconds the co-pilot told air traffic control that they were going to try to get airborne and fly over to the nearby Le Bourget aerodrome for an emergency landing. They never made it.

Engine one suddenly lost power and a few seconds later F-BTSC crashed into a hotel at La Patte d'Oie in Gonesse, destroying both itself and the hotel with the deaths of all 100 passengers, nine crew – the three air crew plus three female and two male flight attendants – and four people who inside the hotel. A further six people on the ground suffered minor injuries.

At 2.45pm and 10 seconds the air traffic controller told emergency rescue services on the ground: "The Concorde has crashed near Le Bourget." This was followed a minute later with another announcement: "For all aircraft listening, I will call you back shortly. We're going to get ourselves together and we're going to recommence takeoffs." One pilot from an aircraft waiting to depart told the controller: "There is smoke on runway 26 right, there's something burning apparently." The operator of a runway vehicle said: "There's tyre, pieces of tyre which are burning."

AFTERMATH AND INVESTIGATION

The intense fire which had been engulfing F-BTSC even as it crashed caused catastrophic damage. Even a second hotel near the crash site suffered damage from the resulting high temperature fireball. Firefighters from the south fire station at Paris Charles de Gaulle aerodrome set off for the scene of the crash immediately after being alerted by air traffic control but the first firemen to reach it were from Le Bourget aerodrome. In the face of 94 tonnes of burning fuel they were unable to do anything more than limit the spread of the fire and help the six injured people on the ground.

When the airport firemen arrived with 12 vehicles, including six with foam fire-fighting systems, they pumped more than 180,000 litres of water on to the fire plus 3800 litres of foam. Reinforcement quickly arrived on the scene from neighbouring fire stations but it still took more than three hours to bring the blaze under control.

Air accident investigators were informed at 2.50pm and the inquiry into what had happened got under way immediately. A British representative of the Civil Aviation Authority and two investigators plus technical experts from BAe Systems and Rolls-Royce flew out to France to take part along with German and American observers.

The day after the crash, working groups were set up to find and collect together every possible detail that might be relevant to what happened. They were divided up into seven areas – site and wreckage; aircraft, systems and engines; preparation and conduct of the flight and personnel information; flight recorders; aircraft performance; witness testimony and, finally, examination of previous events.

Preliminary findings of the investigation, published on August 31, 2000, concluded that Concorde's tyre had been cut by a titanium strip which had fallen from the last aircraft to use runway 26 before Concorde – a DC-10 operated by Continental Airlines. After the report had been published, investigators held a meeting with representatives of the firm at its headquarters in Washington. Two further interim reports were then published on December 15, 2000, and July 10, 2001.

The final report gives a detailed account of the fatal crash and the subsequent investigation. Among the most important pieces of evidence it examines are the flight data recorders, of which there were three. The aircraft's Sundstrand flight data recorder had suffered impact damage to its outer casing and showed signs of exposure to fire but internally it was in good working order. The second 'black box', a Dassault Quick Access Recorder, was found to be crushed and its magneto-optical disc was deformed but part of its memory card survived. The third device, the cockpit voice recorder, a four-track magnetic tape recorder, was in good condition.

Smoke billows from the crash site of Air France Concorde F-BTSC in Gonesse, near Paris.

An aerial view of the crash scene.

Poignantly, the voice recorder taped Captain Marty saying to the flight engineer, three minutes before clearance was given for takeoff: "Between zero and 100 knots (115mph) I stop for any aural warning; the tyre flash, tyre flash and failure callout from you, right? Between 100 knots and V1 (a point on the runway) I ignore the gong and I stop for an engine fire, a tyre flash and the failure callout. After V1, we continue on the SID we just talked about; we land back on runway 26, right?"

Point V1 on the runway had been reached 10 seconds before the air traffic controller radioed the crew to alert them to the fire beneath the left wing.

The main focus of the investigation, the metal strip from the DC-10, is described as being "about 43cm long, bent at one of its ends. Its width varies from 29 to 34mm and it has drilled holes, some containing rivets, similar to the Cherry aeronautical type. The holes are not at regular intervals. On visual inspection, the piece appeared to be made of light alloy, coated on one side with epoxy primer (greenish) and on the other side with what appeared to be red aircraft mastic for hot sections. It did not appear to have been exposed to high temperature. This piece was not identified as part of the Concorde".

Examination of the first fire-scorched 6500ft space between the end of runway 26 and the hotel where Concorde ended up revealed a piece of Concorde's left inner elevon, its tail cone anti-collision light, a severely fire damaged inspection panel from the lower wing surface, seven inspection

Firefighters inspect the smouldering debris of the hotel in Gonesse.

panels from the upper left wing with no signs of fire, a fire damaged piece of ducting and further fire damaged structural parts from the aircraft's tail cone.

Beyond this, and right up to the hotel itself, were found pieces of the engine nacelles, bits of wings including parts of fuel tanks, hydraulic lines and shut-off valves and numerous other smaller pieces of debris.

The scene of the crash was divided into a grid and searched by the investigators. They found that the wreckage had been almost completely immolated by the tonnes of fuel the aircraft had been carrying for its journey to New York.

Only the front parts of the aircraft had escaped, along with a few scattered bits of fuselage. When it finally hit the ground, F-BTSC had been practically flat on its belly with very little forward speed remaining and it broke up within a fairly tight area. A large number of parts from the cockpit, including the pilots' seats, throttle levers and autopilot control unit, had hit an electrical transformer near the hotel. The bodies of the pilots were found in their takeoff positions. The nose landing gear, still extended, was found nearby. The passenger cabin was found within what little remained of the hotel structure.

There was no hope of finding any survivors at the crash site. The fireball resulting from 94 tonnes of burning jet fuel was simply too intense.

> **ALL TESTS AND EXAMINATIONS SHOWED THAT CONCORDE HAD BEEN FUNCTIONING NORMALLY WITHOUT ANY PROBLEMS WHICH WOULD HAVE CAUSED SUCH A SERIOUS ACCIDENT – APART FROM THE CUT TYRE AND THE RESULTING DAMAGE TO THE FUEL TANK.**

All the passengers were in their seats with their seat belts still fastened. All four engines were found but none of them showed any sign of fire damage before the crash.

Once all the pieces of wreckage had been identified, recorded and collected, they were taken away and reconstructed as far as possible between October 2000 and January 31, 2001. All tests and examinations showed that Concorde had been functioning normally without any problems which would have caused such a serious accident – apart from the cut tyre and the resulting damage to the fuel tank.

HOW THE CREW REACTED

In assessing the response of Captain Marty and his crew to the disaster unfolding around them, the final air accident investigator's report states: "During the first 38 seconds of the takeoff, the crew were in a perfectly normal situation. Passage through 115mph and V1 was announced without any hint of a problem.

"In the following second, an unusual noise appeared, then almost instantaneously the crew perceived violent lateral and longitudinal accelerations due to the sudden loss of thrust on engines one and two. In the same second, the track deviated towards the left edge of the runway."

It suggests that the crew were particularly conscious of the vital importance of speed during takeoff but: "They were not, however, prepared for a highly unlikely double engine failure on the takeoff run, which is not taken into account in the certification of the aircraft nor, consequently, covered during type rating and crew training.

"As a result, they had no points of reference to identify it and consequently no pre-established solution to face it, apart from dealing with the failure of one engine. The flight engineer, who in this phase of flight mainly devotes himself to overseeing the engine parameters in the central position, certainly noticed the loss of thrust on engines one and two.

"It was probably this which led him to say the word 'stop'. Then, noting that engine one was in a clear recovery phase, he announced the failure with a hesitant verbal communication 'failure eng... failure engine two', which is indicative of his state of agitation."

Here the report states that, had the crew decided to abort the takeoff at this point, the aircraft would have sped off the runway at high speed. Its landing gear would have collapsed and with the fire raging under its left wing it would have burst into flames immediately. As it was, the captain was suddenly forced to apply more force to the controls than he would have expected even in a single engine failure and the crew would have had little time to correctly interpret the sounds and alarms suddenly going off in the cockpit.

The report says: "The accumulation of all of these sensory inputs in such a short space of time led the crew into a totally unknown highly dynamic situation, with no pre-established solution to face it in a phase of flight where, having passed V1, they were mentally prepared for rotation (take off). In this exceptional and unknown environment, the decision to take off as soon as possible appears to have become compelling.

"The crew had no way of grasping the overall reality of the situation. They reacted instinctively when they perceived an extremely serious but unknown situation, which they were evaluating by way of their sensory perceptions. Each time the situation allowed, they applied the established procedure in a professional way."

The last words of Captain Christian Marty and his crew

The black box recorder retrieved from the wreckage of Air France Flight 4590 captured the final moments of the aircraft. The following transcript opens at 4.42pm, local time, on July 25, 2000. Unclear words, sounds and background noises are indicated in brackets.

Control tower: Air France 4590, runway 26 right, wind zero 90 knots, takeoff authorised.
Co-pilot: 4590 taking off 26 right (sound of switch).
Pilot: Is everyone ready?
Co-pilot: Yes.
Flight engineer: Yes.
Pilot: Up to 100, 150 (unclear words, sound of switch). Top (sound of engines increasing power).
Unidentified voice on radio channel: Go on, Christian.
Flight engineer: We have four heated up (sound of switch).
Co-pilot: One hundred knots.
Pilot: Confirmed.
Flight engineer: Four green.
Co-pilot: V one (low-frequency noise).
Pilot: (unclear).
Co-pilot: Watch out.
Control tower: Concorde zero... 4590, you have flames (unclear) you have flames behind you.
Unidentified voice: (simultaneously on radio) Right (background noise changes, sound of switch).
Flight engineer: Stop (unclear).
Co-pilot: Well received.
Flight engineer: Failure eng... failure engine two (two sounds of switches, followed by engine fire alarm going off).
Unidentified voice on radio: It's burning badly, huh (sound of ringing engine fire alarm).
Flight engineer: Cut engine two.
Pilot: Engine fire procedure (sound of switch, end of ringing).
Co-pilot: Warning, the airspeed indicator, the airspeed indicator, the airspeed indicator (sound of switch, ringing alarm sounds again).
Control tower: It's burning badly and I'm not sure it's coming from the engine (switch sound, possibly engine fire extinguisher handle being activated).
Pilot: Gear on the way up.
Control tower: 4590, you have strong flames behind you.
Flight engineer: The gear (toilet smoke detector alarm sounds).

Control tower: Beginning reception of a middle marker.
Co-pilot: Yes, well received.
Flight engineer: The gear, no (sound of ringing engine fire alarm).
Control tower: So, at your convenience, you have priority to land.
Flight engineer: Gear.
Co-pilot: No (two switch noises).
Pilot: Gear (unclear), coming up.
Co-pilot: Well received (fire alarm, gong, three switch sounds).
Co-pilot: I'm trying (unclear).
Flight engineer: I'm hitting.
Pilot: Are (unclear) you cutting engine two (end of smoke alarm)?
Flight engineer: I've cut it.
Control tower: End reception middle marker.
Co-pilot: The airspeed indicator (sound of switch, end of ringing alarm).
Co-pilot: The gear won't come up (fire alarm rings).
Aircraft instrument: Whoop whoop pull up (repeats).
Co-pilot: The airspeed indicator.
Aircraft instrument: Whoop whoop pull up.
Fire service leader: De Gaulle tower from fire service leader.
Control tower: Fire service leader, uh... the Concorde, I don't know its intentions, get yourself in position near the south doublet (sound of switch).
Pilot: (unclear).
Fire service leader: De Gaulle tower from fire service leader authorisation to enter 26 right.
Co-pilot: Le Bourget, Le Bourget, Le Bourget.
Pilot: Too late (unclear).
Control tower: Fire service leader, correction, the Concorde is returning to runway zero nine in the opposite direction.
Pilot: No time, no (unclear).
Co-pilot: Negative, we're trying Le Bourget (four switching sounds).
Co-pilot: No (unclear).
Fire service leader: De Gaulle tower from fire service leader, can you give me the situation of the Concorde (two alarms and sound of switch, followed by another switch and sounds likened to objects being moved).
Pilot: (unclear).
Recording ends.

French firemen look through debris at the crash site.

Debris from the nose and cockpit of F-BTSC.

The 16in metal strip found on the runway at Paris Charles De Gaulle airport after the Concorde crash. It was later determined that this had sliced a cut right across one of the aircraft's tyres.

THE METAL STRIP

Crash investigators were highly critical of the runway inspection process at Paris Charles de Gaulle in the wake of the Concorde crash. Their report states: "It is also notable that, as far as Paris Charles de Gaulle is concerned, the daily average was limited to two inspections whereas a service memo specified three, which shows that these inspections are not a priority when faced with operational constraints.

"The manner in which the discovery of debris is handled is equally unsatisfactory. Thus, at ADP (the Paris Airports Authority), items discovered on the manoeuvring area are simply noted in a log and sometimes information is passed on to the operator and the BEA.

"There is no systematic research to determine the origin of the debris and the indicator boards which are the basis for safety follow-up contain no data on this question. As to the apron, there is no follow-up, either qualitative or quantitative, of the presence of debris though there is a body for co-ordination with airport users, accompanied by awareness and training campaigns."

It emphasises the importance of establishing a better means of ensuring that debris is removed from runways and states that the metal strip which caused the Concorde crash should have been spotted and removed.

"The investigation did however show the limits of the means currently employed in this area," it states. "The metallic strip that led to the destruction of the tyre had been lost from an aircraft that had taken off five minutes before the Concorde. It seems inconceivable, bearing in mind current traffic at large aerodromes, to base a policy on prevention of risks related to debris on inspections alone.

"To increase their frequency could of course improve the detection of foreign bodies, but that would remain limited to aerodromes with light traffic and appears impractical at aerodromes such as Paris Charles de Gaulle. For the latter, takeoff and landing frequencies are such that there is practically an aircraft permanently on the runway, with a consequent increase in the risk of lost parts, where only a permanent automatic detection system would ensure satisfactory surveillance. Installation of appropriate equipment would, additionally, allow precious information to be made available in case of accidents occurring during takeoff and landing phases."

Sifting through the wreckage after the crash.

COURT ACTION

On December 6, 2010, Continental Airlines and John Taylor, one of its mechanics, were found guilty of involuntary manslaughter, but on November 30, 2012, a French court overturned the conviction, saying mistakes by Continental and Taylor did not make them criminally responsible.

Prior to the accident, Concorde had been considered the safest operational passenger airliner in the world in terms of passenger deaths-per-kilometres travelled. Safety improvements were made in the wake of the crash, including more secure electrical controls, Kevlar lining to the fuel tanks and specially developed burst-resistant tyres.

It seemed that the dream was over however. The investigations and recriminations went on and on for months but eventually the problem that would not go away had to be faced. Could Concorde take to the air again or was that it? The first flight after the modifications departed from Heathrow on July 17, 2001, piloted by BA

ABOVE RIGHT: An investigator inspects remnants of a crashed Concorde supersonic jet in a hangar in Dugny, north of Paris, in November 2000.

RIGHT: British Airways Concorde flight BA003 which was cancelled at London Heathrow International Airport after an Air France Concorde crashed soon after take-off from Charles de Gaulle airport, with the loss of 109 lives.

RIGHT: A British Airways Concorde modified in the wake of the Air France Concorde crash arrives at Shannon Airport in the Republic of Ireland for flight crew refresher training. The flight from London's Heathrow airport followed two successful verification flights out into the Atlantic by the same aircraft.

> **THE INVESTIGATIONS AND RECRIMINATIONS WENT ON AND ON FOR MONTHS BUT EVENTUALLY THE PROBLEM THAT WOULD NOT GO AWAY HAD TO BE FACED. COULD CONCORDE TAKE TO THE AIR AGAIN OR WAS THAT IT?**

Chief Concorde Pilot Mike Bannister. It lasted nearly three and a half hours during which time the aircraft was taken over the mid-Atlantic towards Iceland. Captain Bannister hit Mach 2.02 and 60,000ft before returning to RAF Brize Norton. The test flight, intended to resemble the London to New York route, was declared a success.

There was now nothing to stop commercial flights resuming and the first operation with passengers after the accident took place on September 11, 2001. It was a dress rehearsal of sorts – all those on board were BA employees – but the terrorist attacks on New York quickly put a halt to any plans for Concorde's return to the city.

Normal commercial operations resumed on November 7, 2001, but the writing was already on the wall. On April 10, 2003, Air France and British Airways simultaneously announced that they were intending to retire Concorde. They both cited low passenger numbers following the July 2000 crash, the general slump in air travel following the American terrorism attacks on September 11, 2001, and rising maintenance costs.

On the same day as the retirement announcement, Sir Richard Branson offered to buy British Airways' Concorde fleet at their "original price of £1" for service with his Virgin Atlantic Airways. Sir Richard made the offer claiming this was the same token price that British Airways had paid the British government.

British Airways was quick to deny the claim and refused the offer. Branson later wrote in The Economist magazine that his final offer was actually "over £5 million" and that he had intended to operate the fleet "for many years to come".

There have been a number of further offers to revive the Concorde fleet over the years since then but all have come to nothing. It seems that the cost of bringing the highly complex aircraft back into service after 10 years away is now simply insurmountable and as such Concorde may never fly again.

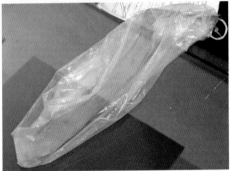

RIGHT: The metal strip that fell from a Continental DC-10 bagged up as evidence in Continental's trial.

BELOW: Lawyer Olivier Metzneras delivers a statement to the media after the conclusion of the Air France Concorde crash court case.

Air France Concorde F-BTSD pictured in 1978.

What Concorde meant to the French

Gallic pride, determination and technological prowess

Concorde was a potent symbol of design and engineering innovation on both sides of the English Channel and the French were just as proud of the end result as their British counterparts. Building Concorde was also an exercise in building trust and cooperation between the two nations' aviation industries, which had formerly been rivals. In the end, the spirit of friendly competition resulted in a better aircraft.

CHAPTER SEVENTEEN

Japanese journalists study an Air France Concorde after its first fight from Paris to Kansai International Airport near Osaka, Japan, on September 5, 1994, marking the airport's official opening.

When Britain and France signed a treaty agreeing to build a supersonic airliner together in November 1962, the pride of both nations was at stake. France had just become a nuclear power, the European Economic Community (EEC) was being forged with France at its heart and President Charles de Gaulle was determined to demonstrate that his nation was just as much a world superpower as the US or Britain.

While de Gaulle disliked having to work alongside the British he accepted it as a financial necessity and was determined the project should succeed. Even when he gave the speech that vetoed Britain's membership of the EEC on January 14, 1963, he was careful to mention the two nations' "direct cooperation in all kinds of fields, and notably the scientific, technical and industrial – as the two countries have just proved by deciding to build together the supersonic aircraft Concorde".

This was actually the first time the name Concorde had been formally used for the project, having first been picked out of a Roget's Thesaurus by a BAC executive while discussing the aircraft at home with his family a few weeks earlier.

The high level of organisation required for the design and construction of Concorde, and the bringing together of two very different aviation industry cultures, generated a degree of friction that initially took time to overcome. The vast sums of money being ploughed into the project by both nations was naturally a lucrative source of revenue for any manufacturing concern that was able to secure a contract. Securing contracts meant extra jobs and wealth so both Britain and France naturally wanted to ensure that they got their fair share.

Concorde engineer Sir James Hamilton, who was responsible for the design of the aircraft's delta wing, said: "There is no doubt that the French saw Concorde as a splendid opportunity to improve the status and standing of their equipment industry. There were a number of components, of which the hydraulic pumps and the generating equipment spring most readily to mind, where if this had been an aeroplane designed by a single country, there would not have been anything like the number of changes that were made. Those were the worst two examples.

"On the hydraulic pumps, I remember very clearly, what happened was that a British firm would be chosen for it, but the French would encourage, or not discourage, a French firm in doing a development which was very similar to the Concorde thing, so that they would be sitting there, ready. Then one got a great deal of pressure from the French government saying: 'This hydraulic pump is better than the hydraulic pump you've got, it's more up to date.' Against that, of course, it was at a much earlier stage in the gestation process."

The British Electronic Engineering Association, which represented a number of British aviation component manufacturers was concerned that the sharing of technology with France was teaching the French aviation industry how to build aviation electronics already developed by the British at the expense of British taxpayers. But then the French aviation industry already had considerable skill in manufacturing aircraft equipment and both nations were able to contribute expertise on particular areas of the build.

The Sud Aviation project to create a Super Caravelle airliner had been founded upon knowledge and experience built up during the development of aircraft such as the phenomenal delta-winged Mirage III fighter, which entered service in 1961. Concorde's silhouette as seen from below is not entirely dissimilar from that of the Mirage.

Some believed that the French viewed Concorde as a prestige project that would demonstrate the dominance of their aviation technology over other European nations. BAC Concorde engineering director David Farrar said: "The fundamental objectives of the British and French companies were different. The British wanted a viable, economic supersonic transport aircraft of transatlantic range. The French merely wanted a transatlantic range aircraft with a specified payload and advanced technology. After 1965 the British government felt bound to continue under the terms of the agreement, although clearly embarrassed by mounting costs and programme slip. The French just pressed on, as far as I could see, with their original objectives. The French technical direction of the entire aircraft from Sud did the same, belatedly accepting improvements to the payload proposed by the British. The BAC Filton objective was, I think, team survival. The Sud objective was European domination."

This was not necessarily how the French themselves saw the situation. As French newspaper Liberation put it: "Not only did Concorde embody a certain conception of a victorious France, above all it symbolised modernity – triumphant in all the refined elegance of its curves. The technical achievement was also an aesthetic marvel, binding form and function in a single line."

For French Minister of Transport and Public Works, Edgard Pisani, speaking to an audience of British aerospace company executives in September 1966, Concorde had a somewhat more practical and less poetic purpose.

"The primary aim for you, as for us, is to keep this industry alive," he said. "For technological, commercial and also political reasons, our countries cannot allow themselves to sink to the level of mere subcontractors. Here is the basic reason and justification, in our view, for the present programme of civil and military cooperation materialised in the Concorde project."

The last flight of an Air France Concorde F-BVFB ends at the Karlsruhe-Baden-Baden airport in Soellingen-Rheinmuenster, Germany. The aircraft is now on display at the Technique Museum at Sinsheim, close to Stuttgart.

Whatever the differences between the British and French teams, they managed to work together on a project the like of which the aviation industry had simply never seen before. Both teams were passionate about getting it right and this dedication helped to ensure that when Concorde did eventually reach airline service it successfully represented the combined skills and knowledge of both nations.

Sir Archibald Russell, whose work with Bristol in the late 1950s had made Concorde possible, and who was joint chairman of the Concorde Executive Committee of Directors between 1965 and 1969, said: "Every bloody thing the French would put

forward we'd do our best to knock it down, and everything we put forward they'd do their best to knock it down. So you couldn't get by with a loose proposition.

"And I think I must put part of the credit for the eventual technical success down to the fact that there was no possibility of a loose decision getting through."

British Airways and Air France had a less formal relationship in operating Concorde than the relationship that had existed between BAC and Sud during the aircraft's construction but it was generally one of friendship and cooperation rather than of competition. For example, during his time as British Airways Concorde

Air France Concorde F-BVFA sits on the Tarmac of Logan International Airport in Boston, US, on January 17, 1987. It was diverted there after reporting a low fuel supply and smoke in its cockpit.

project director, Gordon Davidson maintained close contact with his opposite number at Air France, Jean-Claude Martin. As a result, British and French Concorde operations often overlapped, such as the when the Braniff services operating in the US utilised both British and French Concorde aircraft.

The crash in 2000 hit Air France hard and many of its staff were saddened by both the accident and what happened to Concorde afterwards.

Air France load master Martine Tlouzeau recalled the return to Paris of Concorde F-BVFC after it had been grounded at JFK following the fatal crash of sister aircraft F-BTSC in 2000.

She said: "F-BVFC had been grounded at JFK since July 25 and finally got the authorisation to return to Paris on September 21. I don't think any Air France staff on duty that day would have missed the opportunity to escort our wonderful white bird along the taxiway to his last stand at the maintenance area. It was an occasion for us to say how much we loved him and how much we missed him too.

"Some of us were gathered on the Romeo de-icing area which offers a nice view of Runway 27 where Concorde was supposed to land. At 3.27pm, the familiar shape appeared in final approach, lights on. Three minutes later Concorde landed, perfect and majestic, as usual, and so silent... I have been told, afterwards, a lot of drivers stopped their cars along the A1 highway to watch the Concorde land and a great traffic jam occurred. The weather which was so bright and sunny a couple of

hours earlier had turned cloudy and grey. It started to rain, as if the weather wanted to show its sorrow too. Concorde left Runway 27 and started his last goodbye tour. He got the authorisation to make a special farewell loop to terminal 2 before going to the maintenance for a while or forever.

"As we were waving to the crew the co-pilot opened the cockpit window and responded, waving his hand to our small group, then the emotion turned so strong that the tears started to mix with the rain on our faces. Concorde went on to his rendez-vous in front of the headquater building.

"We followed him and rejoined him precisely when he stopped for a little while in front of the building to thank hundreds of persons who came out, under the rain, to show him how much they care for him. I couldn't see it but the Captain threw a rose from the cockpit in memory of the 113 victims. Someone had written "Concorde je t'aime" on a banderole.

"Most of the staff was gathered here, and this was another great moment of emotion. I had the feeling I was living an historical moment, and Concorde will never fly again and I feel so sad."

Air France's final scheduled Concorde journey to New York began in Paris on Friday, May 30, 2003.

Flight AF002 was waved off for the final passenger trip to New York from Terminal 2 at Paris Charles de Gaulle for the three hour 45 minute flight to JFK. Ahead of the flight,

the Air France Concorde staff team leader Sebasrian Weder said: "It was our life – every day of it – and from May 31 there will be a great void."

Captain Jean-Louis Chatelain, who had flown Concorde regularly since 2001, said: "Every flight is a moment of delight. It is the Formula One of aviation – with the performance of a jet fighter on a civil transport."

In the cabin, chief flight attendant Joelle Cornet-Templet enthused: "It is a magic aircraft. The pleasure of flying in it is almost a carnal one."

The following day, the aircraft, F-BTSD, returned to Paris Charles de Gaulle. One passenger said: "In France we don't know how to hold on to what is beautiful."

Air France chairman Jean-Cyril Spinetta said: "Concorde will never really stop flying because it will live on in people's imaginations."

The flight touched down at 5.44pm. Several thousand more Concorde fans inside the airport greeted the 'white bird'. As the aircraft made its way along the taxiway some held banners reading: "Thank you Concorde, we love you."

French Transport Secretary Dominique Bussereau said: "It is the end of an era in aviation."

The last farewell
Final commercial flights

With the decision made to withdraw Concorde from service, it only remained to decide how British Airways would say goodbye to the aircraft that had brought it so much joy and heartache over the years.

A date was set for the end of Concorde's commercial flight with British Airways – October 24, 2003 – and it was decided that the schedule should be arranged so that three Concorde aircraft landed at Heathrow in London in quick succession.

These would be G-BOAE flown in from Edinburgh by Captain Andy Baillie and Captain Les Brodie, G-BOAF flown by Captain Paul Douglas on a round-the-bay trip out of and into Heathrow and the final flight from New York, BA002, operated by G-BOAG with Chief Concorde pilot Mike Bannister and Senior Flight Officer Jonathan Napier at the controls.

They would land one after the other shortly after 4pm, with G-BOAE first followed by G-BOAF and then G-BOAG.

Before stepping into the cockpit, Bannister said he was "proud and privileged" to be the captain of Concorde's last trip back from New York and added: "What we have tried to do is to make the retirement of Concorde a celebration –

Five Concorde aircraft on the Tarmac at Heathrow after the type's last scheduled flight.

CHAPTER EIGHTEEN

Sir David Frost was among Concorde's last passengers, having been one of the aircraft's most frequent flyers over the years.

Darkness descends as two Concorde aircraft come in to land at the same time. And for the last time. **Tim Callaway**

something that both the public and the airline can look back at with pride.

"When I power the engines for the last time at Heathrow I shall be thinking of all the people in British Airways who've kept this plane flying successfully for 27 years."

BA chief executive officer Rod Eddington said that the events of October 24 would be conducted with a "mixture of sadness and celebration".

"It is a wonderful plane, an icon, but its time has come," he said. "It's an old plane – it doesn't look it – but it was designed in the Fifties and built in the Sixties."

Before it took to the air, ground crew at JFK sprayed G-BOAG with jets of red, white and blue water to symbolise the national colours shared by Britain, America and France.

The New York flight left at 12.35pm, G-BOAE left for Edinburgh at 10.35am, landed at noon, and began its return flight at 2.20pm. G-BOAF began its loop of the Bay of Biscay a few minutes after that.

Cabin service director Claire Sullivan wipes away a tear on the last commercial flight of Concorde from JFK to Heathrow.

Two flight attendants hug each other after Concorde's last commercial trip.

Three British Airways Concordes taxi on the runway at Heathrow Airport on October 24. Thousands of people gathered at the airport to see the aircraft land one after the other.

On board G-BOAG, broadcaster Sir David Frost said he had lost count of the number of times he had been on Concorde, adding: "I think it's very sad it's all coming to an end. This last flight is a great experience and there will be a lot of emotion.

"Concorde was the only way to be in two places at the same time. You could be in London at 10am and you could be in New York at 10am on the same day."

Sitting close by, model Jodie Kidd said: "I always really love the rush of takeoff. I am just a speed freak. I'm going to miss it, there's nothing like Concorde."

Ballerina Darcy Bussell said: "I first went on it 10 years ago. We were filming in Paris and I had to get to New York quickly. It was amazing and I never thought I would go on it again."

Jeremy Clarkson, who was also on the flight, later quoted her as saying: "Why can it not be run at a loss? The National Ballet is."

Recalling the experience later, Clarkson himself wrote: "What I feel sorry for is the machine itself. For 27 years, it's flown back and forth across the Atlantic, never putting a foot wrong. And then one day, no-one came to its hangar to hoover its carpets, or replenish its fuel tanks. One day, for no reason that it could possibly understand, its owners decided they didn't want it any more.

"I don't want to sound soft, but think how your dog would feel if you did that: tickled its tummy and filled its bowl for 27 years and then one day, locked it in a kennel and never went back."

Among the other famous faces on that last fight were Formula One magnate Bernie Ecclestone, American actress Christie Brinkley, advertising company director Lord Saatchi, newspaper editor and chat show host Piers Morgan, actor Nigel Havers, BA chairman Lord Marshall and Lord Sterling, chairman of P&O.

During the journey, Bannister made a further announcement: "We have reached the magic number that Concorde was designed to achieve – Mach 2, or 1350 miles per hour."

Reuters also quoted him as saying: "Concorde was born from dreams, built from vision and operated with pride. Concorde is a fabulous aircraft and it has become a legend today."

And as the flight came to an end he said: "Ladies and gentlemen, thank you very much for flying British Airways Concorde."

Passenger Joan Collins, in a diary piece for The Spectator, wrote: "As we approached

Firefighters douse Concorde in an old tradition brought into effect for the end of an aircraft's service career. **Tim Callaway**

Model Jodie Kidd on board the last commercial flight of Concorde from JFK to Heathrow.

Captain Mike Bannister (right) and Senior First Officer Jonathan Napier wave from the cockpit after the final British Airways Concorde journey.

Champagne in hand, motoring writer Jeremy Clarkson prepares for the last commercial Concorde flight.

Heathrow, the announcement brought a sense of solemnity through the cabin. Everyone fixed their gaze intently out of the windows, seeing London pass underneath, cars stopping on the M4 and people waving at us from fields.

"The flight attendants walked down the aisle, bidding godspeed to the regular faces they had become so accustomed to seeing once or twice a week on that New York-London run, thanking them for the memories shared. Everyone felt slightly choked up when we landed, seeing those hundreds of thousands of people who had turned out to say goodbye to their favourite airplane. It was a truly memorable experience."

On the ground there were hundreds of spectators straining to get a good look at the aircraft as they were taxied in. Basingstoke man John Cowburn brought his own ladder to get a decent view. He said he had seen Concorde fly on 25 previous occasions. "Today is a very sad day but we must make the most of it," he said. "Concorde is potentially the most special thing man has ever built."

The sun finally sets on Concorde. **Tim Callaway**

G-BOAD is moved into position at the Intrepid Sea-Air-Space Museum on board the *USS Intrepid* in New York.

WEEKS MARINE

BRITISH AIRWAYS

Where are they now?

From Mach 2 to museum showpiece

There are 18 surviving Concorde aircraft and 15 of them are on public display, though they are not all open to the public. The other three are in storage, two in Britain and one in France, and the surviving parts of a further Concorde are located close to an airport runway in France. The remains of the 20th Concorde are most definitely not available for public viewing.

001 F-TWSS

Current location: Museum of Air and Space, Le Bourget, France
Details: The museum is located at the south-eastern edge of Le Bourget Airport, north of Paris, and in the commune of Le Bourget. From April 1 to September 30, it is open Tuesday to Sunday from 10am to 6pm. From October 1 to March 31 opening times are 10am to 5pm. Closed on Mondays and from December 25 to January 1.
Notes: The first Concorde to be retired and put in a museum. Last flew on October 19, 1973, while being delivered to the museum. Now sits in a dedicated Concorde Hall opposite production Air France Concorde F-BTSD with their noses side by side.

002 G-BSST

Current location: Fleet Air Arm Museum, Yeovilton, England
Details: The museum is near Ilchester, Somerset BA22 8HT, and is open all year round except on December 24-26. From April 1 to November 3 it is open daily from 10am to 5.30pm with last admissions at 4pm. From November 4 to March 31 it is

open from 10am to 4.30pm with last admissions at 3pm.

Notes: Last flew on March 4, 1976, during its delivery flight to Yeovilton. At the Fleet Air Arm Museum, G-BSST sits next to two of the aircraft used during its development – the converted Fairey Delta II, now BAC 221, and the Handley Page HP.115 which was used to test the low speed handling characteristics of a narrow delta wing. In the same hall are the Hawker P.1127 Harrier prototype, a Hawker Hunter T8M, Bristol Scout D, a Wessex HU.2, a Sea Harrier and a de Havilland Vampire T22.

101 G-AXDN

Current location: Imperial War Museum, Duxford, England

Details: IWM Duxford is just south of Cambridge at Junction 10 of the M11 motorway. Parking is free. It is open all year round from 10am except on December 24-26. From March 16 to October 26 it closes at 6pm with last admissions at 5pm. From October 27 to March 14 it is open until 4pm with last admissions at 3pm.

Notes: Flown to Duxford on August 20, 1977, and now resides in the museum's AirSpace exhibition hall alongside a TSR.2, an Avro Vulcan B.2 and numerous other types. It is possible to climb inside G-AXDN and view the cockpit, albeit from behind a rope, and walk down the length of the fuselage.

102 F-WTSA

Current location: Musée Delta, Orly Airport, Paris, France

Details: While the museum, at 40 Avenue Jean Pierre Bénard, 91200 Athis Mons, was closed at the time of going to press, F-WTSA could still be visited from Wednesday and Saturday between 2.30pm and 5.30pm.

Notes: Flown to Orly on May 20, 1976, from Toulouse. F-WTSA is stored out in the open alongside a Mirage fighter jet prototype, a Caravelle airliner, delta-winged piston-engined oddity the PA 100 and a Mercure 100 airliner.

201 F-WTSB

Current location: Airbus Factory, Toulouse, France

Details: The factory is on the Jean Luc Lagardère site in the AeroConstellation aeronautical activities zone, to the north-east of the Toulouse-Blagnac airport. Guided tours currently available six days a week, closed on Sundays and bank holidays. Search 'airbus factory tour' online for more details.

Notes: At present, F-WTSB is only available to view if you take the extended version of the Airbus A380 assembly line tour, but it is expected to form a central exhibit of the new Aéroscopia Museum due to open in 2014.

Visitors walk past Concorde G-BOAA at the National Museum of Flight in Scotland.

The first British production Concorde, G-BBDG, at Brooklands in Weybridge, Surrey.

It took the low road. G-BOAA travels down the Thames on part of its journey to the National Museum of Flight in Scotland.

202 G-BBDG

Current location: Brooklands Museum, Weybridge, Surrey, England
Details: The museum is located between Weybridge and Byfleet, off Junction 10 of the M25 and the A3 London-Portsmouth trunk road. Open every day except December 23-27. Summer opening times are 10am to 5pm and winter is 10am to 4pm. 'Summer' and 'winter' are defined by the start and end of British Summer Time. No dogs allowed and children under 16 must be accompanied.
Notes: Brooklands offers the most comprehensive 'Concorde experience' available anywhere. This involves a 35 minute tour through the aircraft's rear cabin which houses an exhibition on the aircraft's design and development and its history in service. After passing through a display of Concorde's seating since 1976, visitors move into the forward cabin which is fully kitted out with British Airways seating. After taking a seat, 'passengers' then experience a virtual flight featuring the voice of Captain Mike Bannister. On the way out photographs can be taken of the flight deck. Advance booking is essential. Brooklands also houses BAC's Concorde simulator, which was used to train pilots. This too is available to the public, although it is not always open and advance booking is, again, essential.

203 F-BTSC

Current location: Destroyed. The last known location of its remains was in storage at Le Bourget.
Details: N/A.

204 G-BOAC

Current location: Manchester Airport Runway Visitor Park, England
Details: The park, which includes a Concorde conference centre, is in Sunbank Lane, Altrincham WA15 8XQ. Opening times vary, visit www.manchesterairport.co.uk for full details.

G-BOAA is escorted overland across farmland from the A1 to its new home at the National Museum of Flight in Scotland.

Notes: The visitor park offers a range of Concorde experiences. The 'classic' tour entails a 40 minute guided tour of the aircraft's passenger cabins. Upgrade to the Concorde Champagne VIP tour and you can also explore the flight deck – a glass of champagne is included. The technical tour allows you to spend an extended period on the flight deck and you can also get underneath the aircraft to view its engines and undercarriage at close quarters. The visitor park is also home to a Nimrod, the forward section of a Monarch Airlines DC-10, a fully restored BEA Hawker Siddeley Trident 3B and the AVRO 146-RJX, the last full aircraft to be manufactured in Britain.

205 F-BVFA

Current location: Steven F. Udvar-Hazy Center of the Smithsonian National Air and Space Museum, Chantilly, Virginia US
Details: The address is 14390 Air and Space Museum Parkway, Chantilly, VA 20151. It is open every day except Christmas Day from 10am to 5.30pm. Admission is free though there is a charge for parking.
Notes: F-BVFA is located in the Boeing Aviation Hangar which features aircraft hung at various levels from its ceiling. Among them are Pitts Special S-1C Little Stinker, a Curtiss P-40 Warhawk and a Vought Corsair. At ground level, besides F-BVFA, you can see Boeing B-29 Superfortress Enola Gay, Boeing 707 prototype 367-80 or Dash 80, the last remaining Second World War Japanese Aichi M6A Seiran float plane, the Boeing 307 Stratoliner Clipper Flying Cloud, the first airliner with a pressurized cabin. Just next door in the James S. McDonnell Space Hangar is Space Shuttle Discovery and a Lockheed SR-71 Blackbird.

206 G-BOAA

Current location: National Museum of Flight, East Lothian, Scotland
Details: The museum is at East Fortune Airfield, East Lothian EH39 5LF. From April to October it is open seven days a week from 10am to 5pm. Between November and March, the museum is only open at weekends, from 10am to 4pm.
Notes: G-BOAA is housed in its own hangar and audio tours of the aircraft are available. Also on show at the museum are an Avro Vulcan B.2A, Blackburn Buccaneer S.2B, Letov S-103, a Nimrod front fuselage, an English Electric Lightning F.2A, a Vickers Supermarine Spitfire LF.XVIe, a de Havilland Dragon, a de Havilland Tiger Moth, a General Aircraft Cygnet, a Messerschmitt Me 163B-1a Komet, a Miles M.18 Mk II and more.

The first pre-production Concorde, G-AXDN, at Duxford. It is now stored inside a hangar with other exhibits and it is possible to climb aboard it and look round.

207 F-BVFB

Current location: Sinsheim Car & Technology Museum, Germany

Details: The museum is located directly next to the autobahn A6 between Mannheim and Heilbronn in Southern Germany. It is open every day of the year from 9am to 6pm, Monday to Friday, and from 9am to 7pm on Saturdays and Sundays.

Notes: F-BVFB has been positioned beside a Tu-144 Charger 30m up on the museum's roof but it is still a walk-through exhibit with access via a staircase. Other aircraft exhibits at the museum include a Canadair CL-215, de Havilland Venom, Fieseler Storch, Heinkel He 111, Ilyushin IL-18 turboprop airliner, Junkers Ju 52, Junkers Ju 87, Junkers Ju 88, Messerschmitt Bf 109 and Tupolev Tu-134. There are also extensive collections of vintage cars and motorcycles, trains and even agricultural machinery

208 G-BOAB

Current location: Heathrow Airport, London, England

Details: In storage and currently unavailable for public viewing.

209 F-BVFC

Current location: Airbus Factory, Toulouse, France

Details: In storage and currently unavailable for public viewing.

210 G-BOAD

Current location: Intrepid Sea-Air-Space Museum, New York, US

Details: The floating museum is located on the west side of Manhattan on Pier 86, 12th Avenue and 46th Street. From April 1 to October 31 it is open 10am to 5pm, Monday to Friday, and 10am to 6pm on Saturdays, Sundays and holidays. From November 1 to March 31, it is open daily from 10am to 5pm including during holidays.

Notes: G-BOAD is displayed with Space Shuttle Enterprise and a range of other aircraft including a TBM Avenger torpedo bomber, an A-12, forerunner of the SR-71 Blackbird, an F-14 Tomcat, an A-4 Skyhawk, a T-34 Mentor trainer, an E-1 Tracer, an F-11 Tiger, an FJ-2/-3 Fury, an F-8 Crusader, an A-6 Intruder, an F3H Demon, an F-9 Cougar and a Piasecki H-25.

211 F-BVFD

Current location: Scrapped but a section of fuselage remains at Le Bourget, France

Details: The fuselage section is at Dugny, close to the taxiways at Le Bourget. It is not currently on public display.

212 G-BOAE

Current location: Barbados Concorde Experience Museum, Barbados

Details: The museum is located next to the Grantley Adams International Airport, eight miles from the capital city Bridgetown. For full details visit www.barbadosconcorde.com

Notes: The museum is essentially a hangar housing G-BOAE with detailed

G-BOAF is manoeuvred into a hangar at Filton airfield, Bristol. The aircraft is currently unavailable for public viewing but is due to become an exhibit of a new visitor attraction.

On its way to the Intrepid Sea-Air-Space Museum in New York, G-BOAD passes beneath the Verrazano Narrows Bridge, at the mouth of upper New York Bay, on November 23, 2003.

A brass band welcomes G-BOAC to its new home at Manchester Airport in 2004. The aircraft is now inside a hangar at the heart of a visitor attraction.

interpretation areas installed around the sides. There are 11 areas in all, tracing the history of aviation in Barbados in addition to telling the Concorde story.

213: F-BTSD

Current location: Museum of Air and Space, Le Bourget, France
Details: The museum is located at the south-eastern edge of Le Bourget Airport, north of Paris, and in the commune of Le Bourget. From April 1 to September 30, it is open Tuesday to Sunday from 10am to 6pm. From October 1 to March 31 opening times

are 10am to 5pm. Closed on Mondays and from December 25 to January 1.
Notes: Sits in a dedicated Concorde Hall opposite prototype Concorde F-TWSS with their noses side by side.

214 G-BOAG

Current location: Museum of Flight, Seattle, US
Details: The museum's address is 9404 East Marginal Way S, Seattle, WA. Except for Christmas Day and Thanksgiving Day, it is open daily from 10am to 5pm. On the first Thursday of each month it is open from

10am to 9pm with free entry after 5pm.
Notes: G-BOAG is displayed outdoors and there are 150 other aircraft to view besides plus Nasa's Full Fuselage Trainer, a mockup of the Space Shuttle's interior which was designed to train astronauts.

215 F-BVFF

Current location: Paris Charles de Gaulle Airport, Paris, France
Details: The airport's location is 95700 Roissy-en-France, France, and the aircraft is on static display outside.
Notes: F-BVFF is essentially a plinthed gate guardian and is inaccessible to the public, although it can easily be seen.

216 G-BOAF

Current location: Bristol Filton Airport, Bristol, England
Details: Filton is now disused and the Concorde at Filton exhibition is currently closed.
Notes: The final flights from Filton, where Britain's Concorde aircraft were manufactured, took place on December 21, 2012. At the time of going to press, the Bristol Aero Collection Trust had received £243,600 in development funding to further its bid for £4.4 million to create a Bristol Aerospace Centre. If it is built, this will bring G-BOAF together with the Bristol Aero Collection and a number of other collections of artefacts and archives which tell the stories of the British aerospace industry, its people and achievements since 1910 when Bristol entrepreneur Sir George White established the British and Colonial (later, Bristol) Aeroplane Company.

Air France Concorde F-BVFF on display outside Paris Charles de Gaulle Airport.

It's unlikely that this sight will ever be seen again. G-BOAF, retired to Filton near Bristol and now in storage, has been kept outdoors for much of the last 10 years and is likely to have suffered corrosion. **Tim Callaway**

Will Concorde ever fly again?

Assessing the condition of the remaining aircraft

During the decade since Concorde last flew, some of the surviving airframes have been meticulously cared for and kept indoors while others have been subjected to the elements and have suffered corrosion. Campaigners such as the Save Concorde group want to see the 'white bird' fly again but is there any hope of that happening?

CHAPTER TWENTY

Another casualty. G-BOAA will never fly again after its wings were cut off for its move to a museum in Scotland.

Concorde hasn't been seen in flight for 10 years, those aircraft that were still in service in 2003 have since been dispersed around the globe. Getting any of them airworthy again would be a truly Herculean task requiring financial investment running well into the millions and thousands of man hours of labour. But it could, in theory at least, be done.

A major first step for any potential restorer would be to work out which airframe would require the least effort to prepare. Twenty Concorde aircraft were made but only 14 entered production service. With the remaining six prototype, pre-production and production test aircraft having been confined to museums for between 28 and 40 years, they can be ruled out of contention as possible flyers.

One of the 14 was destroyed in the 2000 crash in Paris and another was scrapped. That leaves an even dozen. G-BOAA can also be ruled out since, in order to get it to its current resting place at the National Museum of Flight in Scotland it had to have its wings cut off. They were reattached once the aircraft was in situ but their structural integrity is now fatally compromised meaning that G-BOAA can never fly again.

Narrowing the selection down from here is more difficult since all the remaining 11 are largely intact. However, some would require such a substantial amount of work doing to them that, realistically, they can be ruled out. A critical factor is whether modifications were made to the rear wing

spar while the aircraft was in service.

Microscopic cracks were found in the rear wing spar of G-BOAE shortly before the Paris crash and as a result all the aircraft that re-entered service after the accident had to have this strengthened. If a currently grounded Concorde was to fly again this strengthening would have to have been completed beforehand.

This puts G-BOAB, currently at Heathrow, out of contention. It was never modified and is currently in a very poor condition having been stored outside for seven years. Holes were drilled in the fuselage to drain water that had accumulated inside and these would have to be repaired even before the rear wing spar was strengthened. Most of the flight deck has also been removed and would need to be replaced.

Also stored outside have been G-BOAG in Seattle, G-BOAF at Filton near Bristol, F-

BVFB in Germany and F-BVFF at Paris Charles de Gaulle Airport. None of these locations could be described as being consistently warm and sunny and as a result the aircraft are highly likely to have been affected by the weather. Costly inspection and testing would be required. An even worse case is G-BOAD on the flight deck of the former USS Intrepid in New York. While it had the necessary modifications made while it was in service, G-BOAD is likely to have been subject to salt water corrosion. While it was being stored at Floyd Bennett Field in Brooklyn in 2008, the nose was accidentally damaged and had to be patched up with glass fibre.

That just leaves five viable options: G-BOAC, G-BOAE, F-BVFA, F-BVFC and F-BTSD. Of these, it is unlikely that the Smithsonian National Air and Space Museum in the US would be willing to give

Former Air France F-BVFF is now a gate guardian outside Paris Charles de Gaulle Airport. It has been exposed to the elements for 10 years and is unlikely to be economically viable as a restoration to flight project.

Salt water corrosion is a distinct possibility for G-BOAD after its years out on the deck of the USS Intrepid in New York. The aircraft would probably be too expensive to bring back into service.

up its prize exhibit F-BVFA for a restoration project unless it was absolutely guaranteed to be a success. In the current economic climate, this condition is unlikely to be met and therefore F-BVFA can be excluded from the final four.

The current condition of another airframe, F-BVFC, is currently an unknown quantity since the aircraft is being stored by Airbus at its Toulouse factory and is not available for public viewing. This example of Concorde certainly had all the necessary post crash modifications carried out but its condition may have deteriorated over the last 10 years. Alternatively, it could be the

best surviving example of the type. On the basis of this uncertainty, F-BVFC can be pushed to the back of the queue.

Deciding between the three remaining contenders would be difficult. G-BOAC, now kept indoors at a visitor attraction in Manchester was British Airways' flagship Concorde, since its registration carried the initials of BA's predecessor British Overseas Airways Corporation. It is the oldest true production version of Concorde left in existance but its condition remains outstanding. Its systems were actually powered up in 2011 and 90% were found to be in perfect working order. Those that

weren't would apparently take relatively little effort to fix if the appropriate spare parts can be found. Manchester Airport is right next door so little effort would be required to get the aircraft back to a point where it was ready for takeoff.

Possibly in even better condition, and the best of the British Concorde aircraft, is G-BOAG. The aircraft has been in Barbados since retirement with a climate that serves to preserve aging aircraft. Even if that were not the case, G-BOAG has also been under cover during almost all of its time in the Caribbean and is currently very well looked after. Also, access to Grantley Adams

Concorde for sale

With the number of Concorde aircraft that might be returned to airworthy status dwindling, there is now an enormous quantity of spare parts, memorabilia and other bits and pieces either in private ownership or up for sale.

Bonhams and Christies, for example, regularly sell items from or associated with the aircraft. In 2003, Christie's sold an ex-Concorde Olympus 593 engine for £114,000. A set of Concorde crockery with a guide price of £220 sold for £8855 and a genuine Concorde nosecone with an estimated value of £11,300 went for a staggering £354,400. Another nosecone was sold later by Bonhams for £320,000.

The same sale also saw an ice detector head, a sideslip indicator, a Fairchild cockpit voice recorder control unit, a Jaeger fuel pressure indicator, an Elliott Mach number indicator, an Intertechnique tank contents indicator, a set of napkin rings, six sets of salt and pepper mills, an ashtray and many more Concorde items go under the hammer.

In 2007, a Concorde toilet seat sold for £2350 during a sale in Toulouse. Even in retirement, Concorde is still big business.

British Airways flight attendant Emma Ridges holds up a Concorde Jaeger machmeter, which was sold for £28,000 at auction by Bonhams in 2003 – £24,000 more than the guide price.

A Concorde seat auctioned off by Christie's in France in 2003.

International Airport would be straightforward, making the whole process of preparing for a 'first flight' much easier.

Finally, French Concorde F-BTSD at the Museum of Air and Space at Le Bourget has been religiously maintained in top condition. Its nose is regularly moved up and down and its hydraulic system is in excellent condition. There was some discussion about relighting the aircraft's engines in 2010 but this never came to pass. Still, F-BTSD could be the best prospect of them all.

Assuming that G-BOAC, G-BOAG or F-BTSD was chosen for a return to flight

and sufficient money and support could be gathered for the project, the aircraft would have to undergo a D (Major) Check. This would involve removing all of Concorde's major components and carrying out a battery of tests on them, plus a full structural inspection.

Furthermore, the aircraft's hydraulic systems, a complex network of pumps, pipes and valves, would need to be drained, purged and refilled with a silicate fluid called Chevron M2V. This was used on Concorde because it is able to resist temperatures ranging from –60°C to 2300°C. Chevron still exists and is thought

Returning Vulcan XH558 to flight

Campaigners attempting to save Concorde point to the success of the Vulcan to the Sky Trust in getting another highly complex jet aircraft back into service.

Avro Vulcan B.2 XH558 was delivered to RAF Waddington, near Lincoln, from the Avro factory in Woodford, near Manchester, on July 1, 1960.

The Cold War nuclear bomber was in service with the RAF for 33 years and was the last of its kind to be retired when it was flown to Bruntingthorpe Aerodrome in Leicestershire on March 23, 1993, after being bought from the Ministry of Defence by family firm C Walton Ltd.

C Walton kept the aircraft in good condition and in 1997 a group headed by Dr Robert Pleming came up with a plan to return it to airworthy status. The team steadily gathered support between 1998 and 2000 and completed a technical review which demonstrated that the aircraft was in excellent condition. It was estimated that £3.5 million would be needed for such restoration work as was required. Lottery funding was then successfully applied for and XH558 was bought for the nation by registered charity the Vulcan to the Sky Trust in March 2005. Work was begun on the aircraft in August of the same year.

Twelve months later, XH558 was rolled out – 12

years since it had last flown. More work followed and the aircraft's powerful Olympus engines, an earlier version of those installed on Concorde, were fired up for the first time in preservation during August 2007. There followed still more tests on the ground before XH558 finally flew again on October 18. A Permit to Fly was granted on July 3, 2008, and numerous appearances at air shows and displays have followed.

It is hoped that Concorde's restoration, if it was begun, could follow a similar pattern.

The history of Concorde is bound up with that of the Avro Vulcan. Here a Vulcan is seen acting as a flying testbed for the airliner's Bristol Siddeley Olympus 593. It is hoped that the successful process of restoring Vulcan XH558 could be emulated with one of the surviving Concorde airframes.

Vulcan XH558 during an air show. Could a Concorde such as G-BOAC, G-BOAG or F-BTSD enjoy a similar successful return to the skies?

to have a small quantity of M2V still in storage but it is likely that more would have to be produced, probably at quite considerable expense.

None of the three finalists had their M2V drained when they were retired, which means their hydraulic systems have not been exposed to air internally and are all in good condition. Rolls-Royce would have to be involved in the rehabilitation of Concorde's Olympus 593 engines. This would need to be thoroughly tested and run on the ground to ensure their fitness before they could be reinstalled.

There are stores of spare parts available at the Brooklands Museum in Surrey and much of this could be reconditioned for use

on an aircraft being prepared for a return to airworthiness. Location of the aircraft would also need to be considered since the process of restoring the aircraft would require a clean environment that could be used round the clock. Fortunately all of our candidates are based near existing airports which means this is unlikely to be too much of a problem.

In terms of permissions, Airbus would have to reissue Concorde's type certificate, which was withdrawn in 2003. Without this, there is no way that the aircraft could ever return to service. Options for recertification include a return to subsonic flight with no passenger carrying capacity, a recertification as a 'freighter'

with the option of a small number of passengers or full recertification as a passenger aircraft. The latter would be the most difficult and expensive to achieve.

Permission would also need to be granted by the current owner of any airframe being restored. BA retains ownership of all the British-built examples but the Museum of Air and Space at Le Bourget owns its Concorde in the same way as the Smithsonian owns F-BVFA.

Assuming this was granted, the best course of action might well be to establish a charity to oversee the restoration operation and manage the aircraft during its new flying career.

A definite contender. G-BOAC spent five years out in the open at Manchester before being housed in a hangar as the centrepiece of a visitor attraction. However, its systems were brought online in 2011 and 90% of them worked. If any Concorde has a chance of flying again, it could be this one.

SAVING CONCORDE

Ross Mallett set up and became chairman of the Save Concorde Group in 2004. The first few members attended the final Concorde flight into Filton, on November 26, 2003, and distributed leaflets among the crowd. Word spread, and the group began to receive support from ex-Concorde pilots and engineers, people in British Airways and Air France, and contacts in the Civil Aviation Authority. MPs and MEPs, and luminaries such as Sir Terence Conran and Phil Collins, also gave their backing to the campaign.

In 2004, the group began a petition, and took it to events across the country. Members circulated among the crowds who came to see Concorde G-BOAA floated up the Thames on a barge. They collected signatures in shopping centres and on the London Underground too. In addition, they sold merchandise including car stickers, photographs, and prints, much of it produced by the group members themselves.

The campaigners spoke to more than 20,000 people, from former Concorde workers to people who had enjoyed a once-in-a-lifetime flight, to those who just loved watching the aircraft in action. Buoyed by evident public support, the group took its petition to 10 Downing Street on October 22.

Two weeks later, Virgin Atlantic issued a statement saying that it wished to see Concorde preserved "to fly for the nation".

A month later, the group presented a copy of the petition to Airbus UK at Filton, asking for the company's aid in restoring Concorde's Certificate of Airworthiness.

Today, nine years on, the Save Concorde Group is still campaigning to return Concorde to heritage flight. Members believe that the main obstacle preventing a return to flight is British Airways.

The commercial life of the British Concorde aircraft had come to an end in 2003 when the aircraft were retired to museums. BA itself signalled a desire to see one Concorde fly in a heritage capacity, but the company's plan failed to get the support of the holder of the type certificate, Airbus.

The group subsequently submitted a petition to the Government and Airbus (UK) with more than 30,000 signatures on it in the hope that the Government might offer to help with negotiations but so far to no avail.

For more details on the campaign visit www.saveconcordegroup.co.uk

G-BOAF back home at Airbus's Filton facility before its closure. The aircraft is now in a sorry state, at least cosmetically. Rigorous testing would need to be done before it could even be considered for restoration.

Son of Concorde

Building the next generation supersonic airliner

The potential for a Concorde successor was being considered even when the aircraft was still under development and the last four decades have seen ongoing efforts to create a supersonic transport capable of either extreme range or quiet sonic booms. Several firms are still seeking to create a genuine 'son of Concorde'.

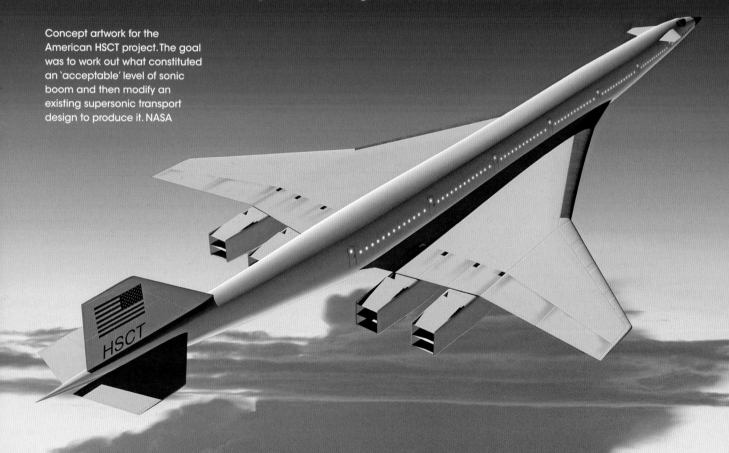

Concept artwork for the American HSCT project. The goal was to work out what constituted an 'acceptable' level of sonic boom and then modify an existing supersonic transport design to produce it. NASA

ABOVE: While pilots of America's next generation airliner would not have been able to see through the windscreen, they would have had a picture of what lay ahead relayed to them from sensors on the aircraft's nose. It would still have been possible to see through the side windows, however. NASA

LEFT: America's future supersonic airliner, as envisioned in 1998, would have had no forward visibility. Instead, the pilots would have watched a digital representation of the view ahead on computer screens. NASA

Even after its 2707 was cancelled and the American SST programme was officially abandoned, Boeing and others never gave up hope that one day supersonic airliners would become a viable business proposition.

NASA in particular has continued to conduct a succession of experiments and tests intended to improve the aerodynamics of faster than sound aircraft to a point where the sonic boom is effectively 'quietened'.

It had been well known since Operation Bongo II in 1964, where 1253 sonic booms were carried out over Oklahoma City in the US over a six month period to test public reaction, that the sonic boom was going to be a problem for any SST.

This certainly proved to be the case with Concorde as several countries either complained about the noise it made going supersonic or refused to allow it permission to pass through their airspace for that reason – effectively limiting its use to overseas routes only.

The earliest work on understanding and mitigating the negative effects of supersonic flight was carried out by German aerospace engineer Adolf Busemann. He presented an academic paper on the movement of air at supersonic speed at a conference in Rome in 1935 but since few aircraft could even travel beyond 300mph at that time his work was largely ignored.

His work continued even as the Second World War shook Germany and some of his research was embodied in the experimental Messerschmitt P.1101 fighter. The prototype of this aircraft was captured by the Americans in 1945 and taken back to the US along, in 1947, with Busemann himself.

It was here, at the National Advisory Committee for Aeronautics facility at Langley, that Busemann began working on minimising the sonic boom effect. His work was taken up by American scientists and engineers whose efforts were made to design an aircraft shape that would enable smoother faster than sound travel.

In 1973, NASA began a programme called Supersonic Cruise Research. This involved extensive wind tunnel testing of various aircraft shapes to study how they would perform at supersonic speeds. It continued until 1982 when its budget was cut by the incoming administration of President Ronald Reagan.

Over in Europe in May 1976, the chairman and managing director of joint Concorde manufacturer Aérospatiale, Jacques Mitterrand, wrote a letter to the British and French governments suggesting that Concorde production could be upgraded to create a 'Version B' that would be far cheaper to produce than Concorde itself since most of the costly development work had already been done.

He further suggested that Concorde B might be the subject of a joint effort between the Europeans and the Americans to reduce the cost still further.

The letter outlined plans for a nine month study looking at the engineering possibilities, the development costs and the

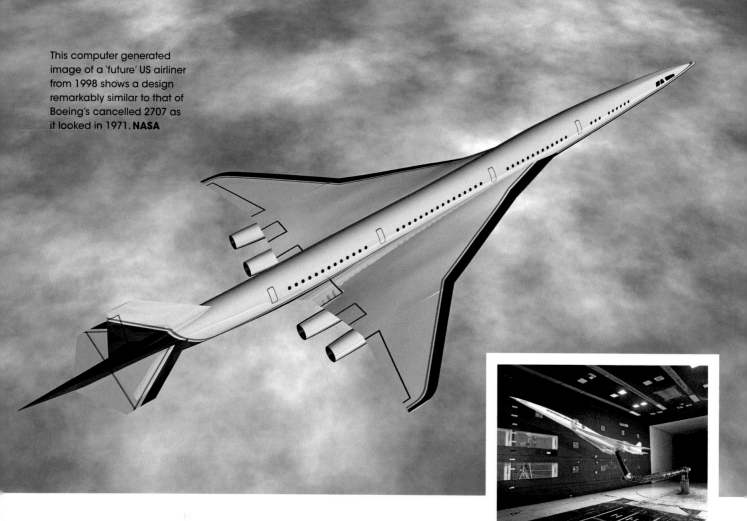

This computer generated image of a 'future' US airliner from 1998 shows a design remarkably similar to that of Boeing's cancelled 2707 as it looked in 1971. **NASA**

potential markets for the new aircraft. If everything went well, a 17th production Concorde could be built by early 1982 incorporating the changes that would result in it becoming a Version B.

The changes would involve reducing the noise produced both during takeoff and landing and at the point of going supersonic. In addition, range would be increased to allow more international routes to be flown.

Range would, it was proposed, be improved by adding 'droop' slats along the leading edge of the wings. The pilot would be able to raise and lower these just like Concorde's nose – drooped down for takeoff and landing to improve lift but raised up for supersonic flight to reduce drag.

This would have the added benefit of reducing the amount of power needed during flight and thereby reducing fuel consumption.

Aircraft's Olympus 593 engines would also be modified to improve fuel consumption at all stages of flight. Their low pressure compressors would be replaced with a model with an increased diameter and their low pressure turbine assemblies would be swapped out for a two-stage turbine.

Airflow would be increased, thrust increased and the reheat system removed, again, cutting noise and the amount of fuel consumed.

Concorde B seemed like a real possibility in 1976 but the still expected orders for the original type never materialised and the 'B' programme was abandoned before it even got off the ground.

NASA'S HSCT PROJECT

After a lull in major research during the early 1980s, the Americans recommenced sonic boom research in earnest in 1988 with the beginning of the NASA High Speed Research (HSR) programme. The organisation brought together a panel of specialists from aerospace firms, the Government and American universities with the stated goal of creating an environmentally acceptable and economically viable overland High Speed Supersonic Commercial Transport (HSCT).

McDonnell Douglas submitted designs to the HSCT programme alongside Boeing. This wind tunnel test model was the result. **NASA**

This would be done by working out what people regarded as an 'acceptable' level of sonic boom and modifying an existing aircraft design to produce it – even if that aircraft design, such as the Boeing 2707, had never actually been made into a working aircraft.

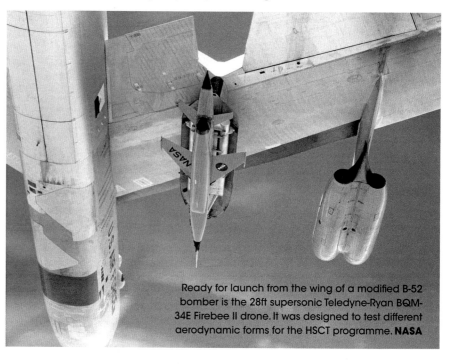

Ready for launch from the wing of a modified B-52 bomber is the 28ft supersonic Teledyne-Ryan BQM-34E Firebee II drone. It was designed to test different aerodynamic forms for the HSCT programme. **NASA**

Fitted with bizarrely asymetrical wings, this F-16XL aircraft was used by NASA to improve laminar airflow on aircraft flying at sustained supersonic speeds. **NASA**

The British Aerospace Advanced Supersonic Transport programme, intended to produce a Concorde successor looking like this, was merged into a joint European project which eventually stalled.

According to a research paper produced for the American Institute of Aeronautics and Astronautics: "In the study, a number of approaches were addressed including the use of non-recoverable supersonic target drones, missiles, full-scale drones such as the QF-4, very large wind-tunnels, ballistic facilities, whirling-arm techniques, rocket sled tracks, and airplane nose probes.

"It was found that the relatively large 28ft supersonic Teledyne-Ryan BQM-34E Firebee II was a suitable test vehicle in terms of its adaptability to geometric modifications, operational capabilities regarding Mach-altitude, availability and cost. The initial program was funded from 1989 through 1992 and included computational fluid dynamics analyses and wind tunnel tests on models of the baseline Firebee II including one in which the vehicle forebody was lengthened by some 40in and reshaped so as to provide a flat-top positive phase sonic boom signature at the ground."

The HSR programme involved manufacturers Boeing, Lockheed and McDonnell Douglas developing and testing high temperature materials, testing structural components for durability and refining construction techniques.

A second phase was launched in 1993 and in December 1995 a single aircraft design was chosen as the focus of the programme. The Technology Concept Aircraft, as it was known, had been evolved from elements of HSCT designs drawn up by Boeing and McDonnell Douglas. It would be a 300 seat Mach 2.4 aircraft with a range of 5000 nautical miles.

There would be no direct forward view for the pilots at all. Instead, external sensors on the aircraft would feed information into its systems to generate a 'virtual view' composed entirely of computer graphics displayed on screens.

A Boeing 737 was modified to incorporate the eXternal Vision System

(XVS) and, with its forward and side windows removed, was used to conduct 20 test flights between November 1995 and January 1996 from NASA's Langley and Wallops Island facilities.

It flew with a BAC 1-11 which was used to test avionics.

During the first phase, they flew typical airport landing approaches and holding patterns to see whether the XVS would pick up other aircraft and objects on the ground. Next, the pilots flew around 90 approaches and landings in the windowless 737 using just the graphics produced by the XVS to 'see'.

A second series of HSR XVS flights took place from April to June 1997. The researchers concluded that it was entirely possible to safely fly an aircraft without being able to see directly what was going on outside and that combining an artificial view from the XVS display with a 'real world' view from side windows produced the best results.

Also in 1996, an F-16XL aircraft was used by NASA in a programme intended to improve laminar airflow on aircraft flying at sustained supersonic speeds. The data gathered was also fed into the HSCT project.

BRITISH AEROSPACE AST

While all this was going on, the Europeans were beginning to demonstrate a renewed interest in supersonic travel. British Aerospace (BAe) and Aerospatiale signed an agreement to conduct a joint preliminary study into the possibility of a second generation SST, a true 'son of Concorde' in May 1990. This followed independent work by both companies into the idea. The BAe design was called the Advanced Supersonic Transport (AST) and the Aerospatiale equivalent was the Avion de Transport Supersonique Futur, also known as Alliance.

At the time, Sid Swadling, commercial aircraft director of engineering at BAe said that the two firms were aiming to produce

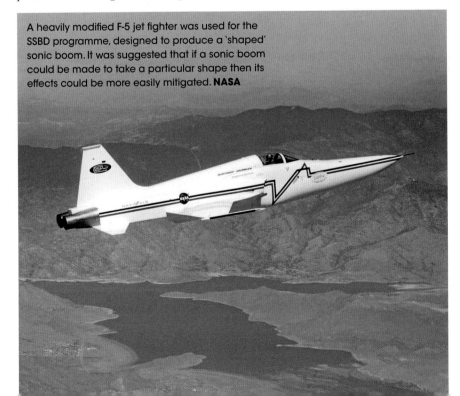

A heavily modified F-5 jet fighter was used for the SSBD programme, designed to produce a 'shaped' sonic boom. It was suggested that if a sonic boom could be made to take a particular shape then its effects could be more easily mitigated. **NASA**

The object on the top of this test rig is one of many proposed shapes for a supersonic airliner being worked on by JAXA, the Japanese space agency.

an aircraft that was 30% better, aerodynamically, than Concorde. On board systems would be based on existing Airbus technology and proposals for the necessary engines would be discussed with General Electric, Pratt & Whitney, Rolls-Royce and SNECMA.

Deutsche Aerospace joined the group in 1994 and a new programme was launched dubbed the European Supersonic Research Programme (ESRP). The ultimate aim was to determine whether producing a Mach 2 airliner with 250 seats and a range of 6300 miles would be a profitable venture.

A report produced by Aerospatiale's aerodynamics department stated: "The technical feasibility of the future supersonic aircraft depends on critical items such as high temperature materials, noise reduction during take-off, low nitrous-oxide emissions,wave drag reduction, weight reduction, artificial vision etc.

"In order to cope with these items, ESRP has been established between the three aircraft manufacturers and their related national research establishments: DLR for Germany, DERA for Great Britain and ONERA for France.

"Within the ESRP project, aircraft manufacturers not only could work with their related national research establishments but also with those from the other countries to give a better flexibility to the project.

"The aim of ESRP is to provide and verify essential technologies for the development of an economically and environmentally viable SCT. Main fields covered within the ESRP are aerodynamics, propulsion integration, structure/materials, systems and technology integration.

"For each of these fields the major issues are addressed to ensure a full coverage of critical items while avoiding unintended

duplication among the various partners.

"Aerodynamics represents 29% of the ESRP activity and if part of the 13.7% contribution from propulsion integration is also included in aerodynamics, it is more than one third of the overall effort that is spent on aerodynamic research for SCT. On the other hand, structure and materials represent 34%, and 16.2% is devoted to the systems.

"Considering that it is a long range aircraft, long overland portions of flight have to be considered. The overland cruise is transonic at Mach 0.95. To cope with this particularity, the ESCT design is optimised both for supersonic and transonic speed."

Supersonic successors summary

AEROSPATIALE/BAC
Aircraft name: Concorde
(for comparison)
Top speed: Mach 2
Range: 4500 miles
Passengers: 100
Current status: Withdrawn from service

BOEING
Unveiled SST designs: 1989 (High Speed Civil Transport)
Unveiled SSBJ study with Sukhoi: 1999
Unveiled current SSBJ design: 2013
Project name: N/A
Top speed: N/A
Range: N/A
Passengers: N/A
Current status: Ongoing

BAE SYSTEMS/ESRP
Unveiled SST plans: 1990
Project name: AST/Alliance/ATSF
Top speed: Mach 2
Range: 6300 miles
Passengers: 250
Current status: On hold

GULFSTREAM
Unveiled SSBJ plans with Sukhoi: 1989
Unveiled current SST/SSBJ plans: 2008
Project name (allocated by NASA): X-54
Top speed: Mach 3
Range: N/A
Passengers: N/A
Current status: Work ongoing

SUKHOI
Unveiled SSBJ plans with Gulfstream: 1989
Unveiled current SSBJ plans: 1999
Project name: S-21
Top speed: Mach 1.95
Range: 5000 miles
Passengers: 6-10
Current status: On hold

JAXA
Unveiled SST designs: 1989
Unveiled SSBJ designs: 2002
Project name: Several designs
Top speed: Various options
Range: Various options
Passengers: Various options
Current status: Work ongoing

Optimistic projections placed demand for such an aircraft at between 500 and 1000 airframes – a prediction which sounded all too familiar to the American predictions of demand for the Boeing 2707 more than two decades earlier.

SHAPED SONIC BOOMS

NASA's HSR programme was moved away from potential production of a Concorde successor in September 1998. A spokesman for the agency said: "What we found out is the technology we were working on was not robust and would not take us to 2010. Rather than focus on configuration technology, we're refocusing on more innovative technological advances." Boeing then left the research programme in 1999. Boeing HSCT programme manager Robert Cuthbertson said: "We knew we could build a one-of-a-kind HSCT prototype. But economically and technically we felt the hurdles were too high to build a commercially viable supersonic aircraft.

"It was clear to us there was still a lot to learn about the manufacturing, particularly with the new materials required. It just wasn't feasible for us to proceed. Until we make more progress in the noise, environmental and manufacturing areas, it's not clear anybody will build a replacement for Concorde."

Just four years later, the Defense Advanced Research Projects Agency (DARPA) launched the Quiet Supersonic

NASA received this Boeing design in 2010. It is seen here in 1.79% scale through the window of NASA's supersonic wind tunnel at the Glenn Research Center in Ohio. **NASA**

DASSAULT
Unveiled SST plans: 1997
Project name: Falcon SSBJ
Top speed: Mach 1.8
Range: 4600-7500 miles
Passengers: 8
Current status: On hold

TUPOLEV
Unveiled SSBJ plans: 2003
Project name: Tu-444
Top speed: Mach 2
Range: 4500 miles
Passengers: 6-10
Current status: Work ongoing

AERION
Unveiled SSBJ plans: 2004
Project name: Aerion SBJ
Top speed: Mach 1.8
Range: 4800-5300 miles
Passengers: 8-12
Current status: Work ongoing

SUPERSONIC AEROSPACE INTERNATIONAL/LOCKHEED MARTIN
Unveiled SSBJ plans: 2006
Project name: Quiet Small Supersonic Transport
Top speed: Mach 1.8
Range: 4600 miles
Passengers: 12
Current status: Uncertain

REACTION ENGINES
Unveiled SST design: 2008
Project name: LAPCAT A2
Top speed: Mach 5
Range: 12,500 miles
Passengers: 300
Current status: Work ongoing

HYPERMACH
Unveiled SSBJ plans: 2011
Project name: SonicStar
Top speed: Mach 3.6
Range: 6900 miles
Passengers: 20
Current status: Work ongoing

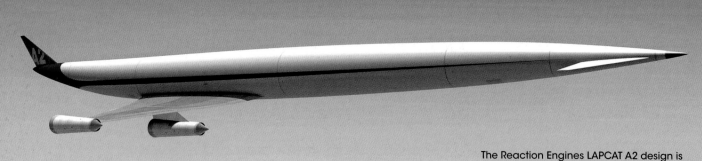

The Reaction Engines LAPCAT A2 design is derived from the firm's Skylon spaceplane – an aircraft that could fly up into space without the aid of rocket boosters. Reaction Engines

Platform (QSP) programme. Ostensibly a military project, this nevertheless had significant ramifications for the development of a future supersonic airliner.

QSP was directed towards the development of an aircraft capable of long range missions with sustained supersonic flight with low takeoff noise and a quiet or even entirely mitigated sonic boom.

The 2003 press release stated: "Highly integrated vehicle concepts will be explored to meet the cruise range and noise level goals. Advanced airframe technologies will be explored to minimise sonic boom and vehicle drag. High performance propulsion systems will be developed to permit long-range supersonic flight with low takeoff and cruise noise levels."

The practical element of this was the Shaped Sonic Boom Experiment or SSBE. On August 27, 2003, a US Navy F-5E fighter dramatically modified by Northrop Grumman demonstrated a method designed to reduce the intensity of sonic booms. An F-15B research testbed jet equipped with measuring instruments recorded shockwave patterns from the F-5E at various distances and orientations. A total of five flights were conducted – three back-to-back with an unmodified US Navy F-5E, and two using the F-15B.

NASA Office of Aerospace Technology vehicle systems programme manager Richard Wlezien said: "This demonstration is the culmination of 40 years of work by visionary engineers. They foresaw a way to solve the sonic boom problem, and to enable a generation of supersonic aircraft that do not disturb people on the ground. It is but one of many frontiers in aeronautics that remain to be explored."

The flight tests showed by designing the aircraft to a specific shape, the pressure waves produced at supersonic speeds could be kept from merging, weakening them. When these weaker waves reach the ground, the loudness of the sonic boom was greatly reduced.

Wlezien said: "The team was confident the SSBD design would work, but field measurements of sonic booms are notoriously difficult. We were all blown away by the clarity of what we measured."

GULFSTREAM AND SUKHOI

American firm Gulfstream and Russian company Sukhoi announced that they would join forces to create a supersonic business jet (SSBJ) in 1989. It was the first time that this new concept had received official backing from any company. In May 1991, Flight International magazine reported: "Gulfstream Aerospace and Sukhoi have agreed a twin engined configuration for their planned supersonic business jet. A model of the twin engined SSBJ will be displayed in the Soviet pavilion at the Paris Air Show in June."

Gulfstream senior vice-president engineer and technology Charles Coppi told the magazine: "The issue is technical readiness. We could put an SSBJ into the air today and it would be just a little bit better than Concorde."

The aircraft was expected to carry between eight and 18 passengers 4600 miles at a Mach 2 cruise speed. Coppi told Flight International that Sukhoi's first design had had three engines and used "Concorde level" technology.

At the time, Gulfstream was said to be "pinning its hopes on NASA work on supersonic laminar flow as a means of reducing cruise drag. Work would also have to be undertaken on engine nozzles since the ones available in 1991 were too noisy. In addition, it was recognised that a traditional windscreen, even one as sharply raked as Concorde's visor, resulted in an aerodynamic penalty. Therefore Gulfstream was "pursuing both synthetic vision, combining television and infra-red sensors, and a periscope system". Finally, the firm was hoping that the HSCT project would "define an acceptable sonic boom signature and to have restrictions on civilian overland supersonic flight removed".

By 1998 it was apparent that the Gulfstream/Sukhoi partnership was over and Sukhoi was making efforts to get another American partner involved, specifically Boeing. At the 1999 Paris Air Show, Sukhoi said that its SSBJ, the S-21, would be powered by three Soyuz VK21 turbofan engines generating 14,500lb of thrust each. It would carry up to 10 passengers and its range would be 5000

miles. At the time, the estimated selling price was £25.5 million to £32 million.

In 2000 it was reported that Sukhoi was attempting to attract interest in the project from Chinese investors and during a discussion in May 2002, Sukhoi general director Mikhail Pogosyan said that progress was being made in cooperation with US firms including a joint feasibility study with Boeing.

It was further reported in 2003 that Sukhoi was in talks with French firm Dassault but it now appears that the project is on hold indefinitely. Gulfstream, however, has continued to press ahead with its plans for an SSBJ.

JAXA

Another SSBJ contender is the Japan Aerospace eXploration Agency (JAXA). The organisation stated in 2008: "Presently, internationalisation of our life, business and industry has made great progress and passenger transport capacity is forecast to become about two and a half times as great as it is now by 2015, and the Asian area will show the highest rate of increase. The appearance of a next generation supersonic transport aircraft with a flight speed twice as fast as that of current large subsonic transport aircraft will result in great strides in international business and sightseeing through the reduction in flying hours.

"JAXA aims to develop a quiet and supersonic passenger aircraft that is more economical and environmentally friendly and expects this to be achieved in the 21st century. We also strive to promote research and development on next generation silent supersonic aircraft technology to establish the advanced technologies necessary for improving economic efficiency and environmental compatibility. This is based on research achievements through the flight experiments of the NEXT-1 project, a small supersonic experimental aircraft project conducted in 2005."

JAXA's ambition, alongside the Society of Japanese Aerospace Companies and the Japan Aircraft Development Corporation between 1989 and 2001 was to create a genuine Concorde successor in the form of an SST which was to carry 300 passengers

5500 nautical miles and reach a cruising speed of Mach 2.2. This was revised down in 2002 to an aircraft which would carry 250 passengers 6000 nautical miles and cruise at Mach 1.6. Its supersonic business jet, possibly called the NEXT-2, would carry 65 passengers 3500 nautical miles at speeds of up to Mach 1.6. JAXA has displayed concept art of how its quiet supersonic business jet could look and as of 2011 it was still working with NASA on testing the necessary technology.

Gulfstream's Quiet Spike sonic boom reducing device takes to the air on NASA's F-15B test aircraft. **NASA**

DASSAULT FALCON SSBJ

French manufacturer Dassault announced that it was working on plans for a supersonic business jet at the National Business Aviation Association convention in 1997. Further details were given at a seminar in Nice, France, in May 1998. The aircraft was to have a double-delta wing and canards and top speed, dictated by its construction from ordinary aluminium alloys, would be in the order of Mach 1.8.

Dassault claimed that its Falcon SSBJ design would reduce the impact of the sonic booms it generated to about half that of those produced by Concorde. There would be no reheat so noise levels during takeoff and landing would be reduced. After two years, in March 1999, the project foundered largely because no suitable engines were available and the cost of developing them from scratch was prohibitive.

It was reported in 2008 that Dassault had signed an agreement with aircraft design testing specialist Onera to work on the potential for a revived SSBJ design. A statement issued on behalf of both firms said: "Our research teams will be working to minimise the drag coefficients of our aircraft to cut fuel consumption. Development of a supersonic corporate jet may also result in joint R&D projects."

THE SECOND RUSSIAN ENTRY

Tupolev's supersonic business jet, the Tu-444, was announced in Russian newspaper Pravda in December 2003. The article outlined Tupolev's thinking in opting to build a small supersonic aircraft rather than a large commercial airliner: "European consortium Airbus announced serial production of the new A380 with 550 passenger seats by 2006. Futurists product 1000 seat planes. At Tupolev such plans are regarded sceptically.

"Airbus will have to have hundreds of orders for such a massive project to break even. They claim, of course, to have some dozens, but it is clearly not enough. A380 would doubtfully be commercially successful. This is why Tupolev has frozen plans for its making similar aircraft of its own. Given the current passenger mass, 10 such planes would be enough for the entire country, and many billions would be lost.

"Tupolev had a project for a similar double-deck airliner of analogous capacity, but it would not be built any time soon due to these financial considerations. Ideas for big, super-capacity passenger planes are not welcomed between Russian aviators. They see the construction of small private supersonic aircraft as much more promising. "This project has already got its name: soon the sky can meet Tu-444, administrative supersonic jets. This business class aeroplane for six to eight people was presented recently in the Czech Republic. At Tupolev, they think that business class jet have a great future, despite their high costs. Tu-444, for example, would be priced around £32 million."

Tupolev's predictions regarding the A380 proved to be somewhat wide of the mark. As of 2013, Airbus has 262 firm orders for the aircraft, of which it has already delivered 103. None of the orders have come from Russian companies however.

Tupolev's own website outlines the need for the supersonic Tu-444 as "more frequent business trips over longer distances and for longer periods of time". It states that its own credentials for developing an aircraft to make these trips come via the development of the Tu-22 Blinder supersonic bomber, the more successful Tu-160 Blackjack swing-

British firm Reaction Engines believes its LAPCAT A2 aircraft design would be the ideal vehicle for its high-tech Scimitar air-breathing rocket engines. Reaction Engines

NASA worked with business jet manufacturer Gulfstream to test its innovative Quiet Spike. This telescoping nose, seen here on NASA's F-15B test aircraft, is designed to dramatically reduce the effects of a sonic boom. **NASA**

wing supersonic bomber and the 'Concordski' Tu-144 Charger.

The firm states: "For the time being, this is substantially the only aircraft plant in Russia and Europe capable of producing thermally loaded, durable structures intended for operation under extreme conditions." It further suggests that the market for the Tu-444 could be in the order of 400 to 700 aircraft as long as it can be produced cheaply enough to bring the price down. The Tu-444 would have a range of 4500 miles and could carry six to 10 passengers depending on the internal layout. It would cruise for limited periods at Mach 2. Recent news updates on the project have been lacking but it is still detailed on the official Tupolev website with performance statistics and artists' impressions, unlike the Sukhoi SSBJ.

THE QUIET SPIKE

In 2006, NASA tested a new Gulfstream device called the Quiet Spike. It was made from a composite material and protruded 14ft from the nose of NASA's F-15B test aircraft during subsonic flight before telescopically extending to 24ft for supersonic flight. It was intended to soften shockwaves spreading out from the aircraft.

Several months of subsonic testing took place before the Quiet Spike was taken on its first supersonic flight in October of that year. This lasted one hour and five minutes at 45,000ft with the aircraft reaching Mach 1.2. Further flights followed with the spike being used up to Mach 1.8. The hope was for the Quiet Spike to change the traditional sonic boom into smooth and more rounded pressure waves, shaped roughly like a sine wave or a sideways S. This resulted in a softer sound that was said to be quieter than the Concorde sonic boom by a factor of 10,000. Gulfstream was continuing its efforts to create an SSBJ, given the name X-54 by NASA, in 2013 having filed a series of patents relating to the project in 2012. The firm is still working to further mitigate the noise produced

by the sonic boom and the designs it filed to the US patent office incorporated the Quiet Spike.

AERION SBJ

American aerospace firm Aerion Corporation is also developing an 'SBJ' design at its base in Reno, Nevada, USA. Its aim is to create an aircraft suitable for offering nonstop travel from Europe to America and back within a day at speeds of up to Mach 1.6.

The predicted price for each aircraft would be around £50 million compared to the cost

of, for example, a Learjet 60 at £8.5 million. Between July and August 2010, and again for eight weeks starting in January 2013, Aerion undertook a series of high speed flight tests in with NASA which subjected aerodynamic models slung beneath the centre line of the F-15B to speeds of up to Mach 2.

Aerion chief technology officer Dr Richard Tracy said: "The Aerion SBJ design utilises patented applications of natural laminar flow for efficiency and speed so understanding the parameters under which such an aircraft will be built and operated is fundamental to proving its viability."

A Lockheed Martin supersonic concept design presented to NASA's Aeronautics Research Mission Directorate in April 2010. At the time it was predicted that the aircraft was unlikely to enter service before 2030-2035. NASA

AMERICAN INTEREST REVIVED

There were reports in 2006 that Supersonic Aerospace International, a company founded by Michael Paulson, son of Gulfstream founder Allan Paulson, had contracted Lockheed Martin to work on a new SSBJ known as the Quiet Small sonic Transport. This aircraft had modest performance ambitions with a top speed of Mach 1.8, a range of 4600 miles and a load of 12 passengers but, crucially, it was to produce only a quiet sonic boom.

Details of the project surfaced occasionally over the following years but in

2010 the Supersonic Aerospace International website became dormant, suggesting that work had ceased. However, Lockheed Martin has continued to produce materials related to supersonic air transport.

In April 2010 it submitted a striking design for a supersonic cruiser to NASA's Aeronautics Research Mission Directorate. Boeing also submitted a design which marked a radical departure from its previous concepts which were largely based on reviving the designs it produced for the 2707 in the late 1960s.

NASA itself unveiled three designs in 2011 for a "widebody airliner that would enter service in 2025 and deliver reductions in fuel and noise emissions". The first, from Boeing, had a blended wing/body shape and was presented in two- and three-engine configurations. The second design was produced by Northrop Grumman and features a huge V-shaped single wing underslung with two long booms to carry passengers or cargo, with the aircraft's twin turbofan engines and a cockpit positioned in between them. The third design, from Lockheed Martin, looks something like a

Concept artwork for the British HyperMach SonicStar design. The SonicStar could reach speeds of up to Mach 4.5 if its American made H-Magjet 4400 hybrid turbofan ramjet engines perform as expected. **HyperMach**

very large conventional airliner body but with wings that loop round on either side to join up with the tail, where the engines are positioned.

Contracts have been awarded to all three firms to investigate their designs' potential with the goal of selecting a single concept for an aircraft to be known as XVT after 2015. If the presumably subsonic XVT is being seen as the future of commercial aviation it could be argued that the future looks uncertain for any potential supersonic airliner. This though, has yet to dissuade the various contenders from pressing ahead with their designs.

BRITISH HIGH-TECH DESIGNS

HyperMach, a firm supported by the British Government, was formed in 2008 to work on a new SSBJ design it calls SonicStar. This Mach 3.6 aircraft would have a range of 6900 miles and would carry 20 passengers, although a second potential configuration of Mach 4.5, 7500 miles and 32 passengers has been mooted.

The SonicStar's performance would be enabled by its engines – H-Magjet 4400 hybrid turbofan ramjets – which are being developed in the US.

HyperMach chief executive Richard Lugg told Aviation International News that the engines included a "superconducting turbo power core ring".

"The first engine stage produces more than 10MW of power, driving the electromagnetic compressor and bypass fans," he said. "There are four turbine stages in H-Magjet, all producing multi-megawatts of power."

The H-Magjet is also expected to 'absorb' the pressure waves from the aircraft's sonic boom, reducing it or even eliminating it.

In December 2011 another British firm, Reaction Engines, outlined how a derivative of its Synthetic Air-Breathing Rocket Engine (SABRE), known as the Scimitar, could be used to give a supersonic airliner a range of up to 12500 miles, halfway around the world, at speeds of up to Mach 5.

The concept aircraft design Reaction came up with to show how the Scimitar would work was called the A2 and was designed in conjunction with phase 2 of the European funded LAPCAT programme. Such a huge range would allow the LAPCAT A2 to operate exclusively over the ocean where it could produce multiple sonic booms without disturbing anyone. Rather than being a small business jet, the A2 would be a 300 seat giant in the mould of the Boeing 2707. The Scimitar engine would work by drawing the oxygen needed for its rocket function from the atmosphere rather than requiring the A2 to carry tonnes of liquid oxygen in an on-board tank.

This weight saving, in the order of 250 tonnes at takeoff, is what makes the A2's other abilities at least theoretically possible. Scimitar would have two modes – the first would see it operating as an air-breathing rocket, sucking in air as a source of oxygen to burn with liquid hydrogen fuel and produce thrust. Using sucked-in air to power a rocket isn't as easy as it sounds since it needs to be hugely

compressed before being injected into the combustion chamber. Doing this raises its temperature high enough to melt any known substance. Scimitar's party piece is a pre-cooler heat exchanger which cools the air so much that it almost becomes a liquid before a conventional turbo compressor is used to compress it. The engine's second mode would see it using a high bypass airflow at subsonic speeds to improve efficiency and reduce noise on takeoff. It seems work on both the Reaction Scimitar engine and the A2 design is ongoing.

Will any of the designs presented here finally result in a new supersonic airliner? All it might take is for a seriously wealthy oil magnate to get involved but whether this will happen is anyone's guess. The wealthy businessmen of Asia might patronise a supersonic service but that's a big 'might' if you're looking at development costs potentially running into hundreds of millions of pounds. Until someone bites that bullet, Concorde will remain the one and only successful supersonic airliner.

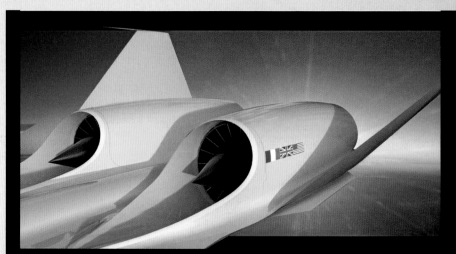

The HyperMach SonicStar's H-Magjet 4400 engines would use superconducting turbo power core rings and would 'absorb' the aircraft's sonic boom. **HyperMach**

Concorde
– the details

CONCORDE DIMENSIONS
(PRODUCTION VERSION)

Overall Length:	202ft 4in (61.66m)
Length from nose to cockpit:	24ft (7.31m)
Height from ground (ground to top of fin):	40ft (12.2m)
Height from lowest point (engine):	28ft 8in (8.9m)
Fuselage maximum external width:	9ft 5in (2.88m)
Fuselage maximum internal width:	8ft 7.4in (2.63m)
Fuselage max external height:	10ft 10in (3.32m)
Fuselage max internal height:	6ft 5in (1.96m)
Fuselage length (flight deck door to rear bulkhead):	129ft (39.32m)
Wing span:	83ft 10in (25.6m)
Wing length (root chord):	90ft 9in (27.66m)
Wing area:	3856sq ft (358.25sq m)
Elevon area (each side):	172.2sq ft (16sq m)
Main gear track:	25ft 4in (7.7m)
Tail fin height:	37ft 1in (11.32m)
Tail fin length (root chord):	34ft 8in (10.58m)
Tail fin area:	365sq ft (33.91sq m)
Rudder area:	112sq ft (10.41sq m)

The first Concorde to be given a new home following its retirement, G-BOAC, takes off from London's Heathrow Airport to travel to its final resting point at Manchester Airport.

Concorde G-BOAB being towed to its final position adjacent to Heathrow's northern runway.

AEROSPATIALE-BAC CONCORDE

Flight crew:	Three – pilot, co-pilot and flight engineer
Flight attendants:	Six (including cabin services director and purser)
Seats:	100 (or 92 in Air France examples after 2001) in two cabins, 40 at the front, 60 to the rear
Maximum weight at takeoff:	400,000lb (181,436kg)
Fuel capacity:	25,250 gallons (119,280 litres)
Fuel consumption:	5638 gallons per hour (25,629 litres per hour)
Range:	3740 miles (5943km)
Cargo capacity:	Up to 1300lb (0.59 tonnes) of cargo
Take-off speed:	250mph (402kph)
Cruising speed:	Mach 2 (1330mph) at 18,288m (60,000ft)
Landing speed:	187mph (300kph)
Power plant:	Four Rolls-Royce/SNECMA Olympus 593 turbofan engines each with a static thrust of 31,000lb
Landing gear:	Eight main wheels (tyres 232psi), two nose wheels (tyres 191psi). The aircraft also has twin tail wheels to protect the rear fuselage and engines though these were seldom needed.
Passenger toilets:	Three (one at the front, two at the rear)
Escape exits with slides:	Six (two at the front, two in the centre over the wings, two over the wings at the rear)
Temperature at Mach 2:	Nose tip 127°C, nose cone 100°C, fuselage 91-98°C, wing leading edge 105°C
Average daily use per aircraft:	2.34 hours
Typical London-New York journey time:	3 hours 30 minutes

SCHEDULED SERVICES
(DURING LATER OPERATION)

British Airways:
London-New York daily
BA 001 10.30-09.25
BA 002 08.30-17.25
BA 003 19.30-18.25
BA 004 13.30-22.25
BA273/2 Barbados (nonstop) once weekly during the winter season and in August.

Earlier services:
Bahrain three times a week
Dallas Fort Worth (via Braniff) three times a week
Miami (via Washington) three times a week
Singapore (via Bahrain) three times a week
Toronto, various schedules
Washington Dulles three times a week

Air France:
New York-Paris
AF001 08.00-17:45 five days per week
Paris-New York
AF002 10.30-08.25 five days per week

Earlier services:
Caracas (via Santa Maria)
Mexico (via Washington)
Rio de Janeiro (via Dakar)
Washington Dulles

CONCORDE DETAILS BY AIRFRAME

Number	Registration	First flew	Last flew	Hours flown	Current location
001	F-WTSS	March 2, 1969	October 19, 1973	812	The Museum of Air and Space, Le Bourget, France

Notes: The French Concorde prototype. Final assembly was begun at Toulouse in March 1966. Rolled out on December 11, 1967. Taxi trials carried out in August 1968. First went supersonic on October 1, 1969, and reached Mach 2 on November 4, 1970. Made a total of 397 flights of which 249 reached supersonic speeds.

| 002 | G-BSST | April 9, 1969 | March 4, 1976 | 836 | Fleet Air Arm Museum, Yeovilton, England |

Notes: The British Concorde prototype. Final assembly was begun at Filton in August 1966. Rolled out on September 19, 1968. First went supersonic on March 25, 1970, and reached Mach 2 on November 12 the same year. Re-registered to the London Science Museum on July 26, 1976. Made a total of 438 flights of which 196 reached supersonic speeds. Kept at Yeovilton on behalf of the science museum.

| 101 | G-AXDN | December 17, 1971 | August 20, 1977 | 632 | Imperial War Museum, Duxford, England |

Notes: The British pre-production Concorde. Initially known as 01 rather than 101 but the three digit code was adopted for ease of use by contemporary computer systems. Differed from the prototype Concorde in having a different wing design, larger fuel tanks, better engines, an improved engine intake system and a glass visor rather than a metal one. First went supersonic on February 12, 1972. On March 26, 1974, 101 reached the fastest speed ever achieved by any Concorde – Mach 2.23 (1480mph). Made the fastest ever east-west crossing of the North Atlantic by an airliner on November 7, 1974, by flying from Fairford to Bangor, Maine, US, in two hours and 56 minutes.

| 102 | F-WTSA | January 10, 1973 | May 20 1976 | 656 | Musée Delta, Orly Airport, Paris, France |

Notes: The French pre-production Concorde. Initially known as 02 rather than 102 but the three digit code was adopted for ease of use by contemporary computer systems. First aircraft to have the final production shape and dimensions of Concorde. First Concorde to visit the US when it attended the grand opening of Dallas-Fort Worth Airport on September 20, 1973. Had British Airways livery on one side and Air France livery on the other for several years but now wears exclusively Air France colours. After retirement to Orly Airport many parts were removed and used as spares for the Air France Concorde fleet. Test equipment was removed and replaced with production style interior seating for walk-through tours. Scheduled to be scrapped in 1988 but this decision was later reversed.

| 201 | F-WTSB | December 6, 1973 | April 19, 1985 | 909 | Airbus Factory, Toulouse, France |

Notes: French production test aircraft. Regarded as a 'production' aircraft it never entered airline service. Flew regularly until 1982.

| 202 | G-BBDG | December 13, 1974 | December 24, 1981 | 1282 | Brooklands Museum, Weybridge, Surrey, England |

Notes: British production test aircraft. Regarded as a 'production' aircraft it never entered airline service. The fastest production Concorde and the first to carry 100 people at Mach 2. Used as a source of spare parts by British Airways starting in 1984. Its nose was used to replace that of G-BOAF when it was damaged during an accident on the ground at Heathrow but G-BOAF's nose was stored, repaired and later fitted to G-BBDG. Moved to Brooklands in June 2004 where it was refurbished and restored before being opened to the public in 2006.

| 203 | F-BTSC | January 31, 1975 | July 25, 2000 | 11989 | Destroyed in crash, Paris, France |

Notes: Originally built as a production test airframe registered F-WTSC, F-BTSC was consequently just under a ton heavier than the other Concorde aircraft operated by Air France. Re-registered as F-BTSC on May 28, 1975. Featured in disaster movie Airport '79: The Concorde in 1979. Stored out of service from 1980 to 1986 when other Air France aircraft were undergoing engineering checks. Carried Pope John Paul II on May 2, 1989. Out of service again between June 1998 and November 1999 while keel beam was replaced due to corrosion at a cost of £4 million.

| 204 | G-BOAC | February 27, 1975 | October 31, 2003 | 22260 | Manchester Airport Viewing Park, England |

Notes: The oldest Concorde on the BA fleet. Initially used on routes to Bahrain and Singapore. Like F-BTSC with Air France, it was also the heaviest Concorde operated by British Airways. Re-registered as G-N81AC/N81AC for service with Braniff Airways in 1979 before being re-registered as G-BOAC the following year. Considered to be BA's Concorde flagship as its registration features the initials of the British Overseas Airways Corporation, BA's predecessor company. Launched BA's Washington service on May 26, 1976.

| 205 | F-BVFA | October 27, 1975 | June 12, 2003 | 17824 | Steven F. Udvar-Hazy Center of the Smithsonian National Air and Space Museum, Chantilly, Virginia, US |

Notes: Re-registered as N94FA for service with Braniff Airways in 1979 before being re-registered as F-BVFA the following year. Flew around the world in 41 hours and 27 minutes in 1998.

| 206 | G-BOAA | November 5, 1975 | August 12, 2000 | 22768 | National Museum of Flight, East Lothian, Scotland |

Notes: Flew the first British Airways service to Bahrain on January 21, 1976 – Concorde's first commercial flight. Also flew the first commercial flight into New York after the city's ban on Concorde was lifted on November 22, 1977. Re-registered as G-N49AA/N49AA for service with Braniff Airways in 1979 before being re-registered as G-BOAA the following year. Flew with the Red Arrows over Heathrow in June 1996 to mark the airport's 50th anniversary. Never fitted with the modifications required in the wake of the Paris crash in 2000. Moved to Scotland by road and sea in 2004.

| 207 | F-BVFB | March 6, 1976 | June 24, 2003 | 14771 | Sinsheim Auto & Technik Museum, Germany |

Notes: Re-registered as N94FB for service with Braniff Airways in 1979 before being re-registered as F-BVFB the following year. Stored between June 1990 and May 1997.

| 208 | G-BOAB | May 18, 1976 | August 15, 2000 | 22296 | Heathrow Airport, London, England |

Notes: Re-registered as G-N94AB/N94AB for service with Braniff Airways in 1979 before being re-registered as G-BOAB the following year. When Concorde flights resumed in the wake of the 2000 Paris crash British Airways only required five aircraft so G-BOAB never underwent the necessary modifications to return to service and never flew again.

| 209 | F-BVFC | July 9, 1976 | June 27, 2003 | 14332 | Airbus Factory, Toulouse, France |

Notes: Re-registered as N94FC for service with Braniff Airways in 1979 before being re-registered as F-BVFC the following year.
Notes: Forced to remain in New York when Concorde was grounded in the wake of the Paris crash in 2000. Flew home two months later.

| 210 | G-BOAD | August 25, 1976 | November 10, 2003 | 23397 | Intrepid Sea-Air-Space Museum, New York, US |

Notes: The only British Airways Concorde to wear the livery of another company, it had Singapore Airlines colours painted down one side in 1979. Re-registered as G-N94AD/N94AD for service with Braniff Airways in 1979 before being re-registered as G-BOAD the following year. Flew during the Queen's Golden Jubilee Flypast on June 4, 2002.

| 211 | F-BVFD | February 10, 1977 | May 27, 1982 | 5814 | Scrapped in 1994. Small fuselage section remains at Le Bourget, France |

Notes: Suffered airframe damage and underwent repairs after landing heavily in Dakar in November 1977. Re-registered as N94FD for service with Braniff Airways in 1979 before being re-registered as F-BVFD the following year. Withdrawn from service in 1982 after Air France ceased its Paris-Dakar-Rio route. Suffered severe corrosion while in storage and was broken up in 1994 at Paris Charles de Gaulle Airport.

| 212 | G-BOAE | March 17, 1977 | November 17, 2003 | 23376 | Grantley Adams International Airport, Barbados |

Notes: Re-registered as G-N94AE/N94AE for service with Braniff Airways in 1979 before being re-registered as G-BOAE the following year.

| 213 | F-BTSD | June 26, 1978 | June 14, 2003 | 12974 | The Museum of Air and Space, Le Bourget, France |

Notes: Re-registered as N94SD for service with Braniff Airways in 1979 before being re-registered as F-BTSD the following year. Holds the world record for the fastest flights around the world in both directions. From October 12-13, 1992, it flew westwards and completed the journey from Lisbon to Lisbon, with six stops in between, in 32 hours, 49 minutes and three seconds. From August 15-16, 1995, it flew eastwards from New York to New York, with six stops in between, in 31 hours, 27 minutes, 49 seconds. Painted in Pepsi livery for a short time in April 1996.

| 214 | G-BOAG | April 21, 1978 | November 5, 2003 | 16239 | Museum of Flight, Seattle, USA |

Notes: First registered as G-BFKW in January 1978 to British Aerospace. Not initially bought by British Airways, G-BOAG had no buyer after being built and ended up being loaned to BA while another of its aircraft was undergoing repairs. Grounded in April 1980 after its hydraulic system was contaminated with water. Finally re-entered service in February 1981 as G-BOAG after £1 million worth of repairs only to be grounded again and used as a source of spare parts until it was returned to service in 1984.

| 215 | F-BVFF | December 26, 1978 | June 11, 2000 | 12421 | Paris-Charles de Gaulle Airport, Paris, France |

Notes: First registered to Aerospatiale as F-WJAN before being re-registered to Air France as F-BVFF on October 23, 1980. First Air France Concorde to travel around the world on a charter trip in 1986. Withdrawn from service in 2000 to become a spare parts source for F-BTSD. Work on getting it back into the air was 60% complete in 2003 when Air France announced the cancellation of its Concorde services.

| 216 | G-BOAF | April 20, 1979 | November 26, 2003 | 18257 | Bristol Filton Airport, Bristol, England |

Notes: Originally registered as G-BFKX to British Aerospace on January 27, 1978, then to the same company again as G-N94AF/G-BOAF on December 14, 1979. Finally re-registered as just G-BOAF on June 12, 1980. First Concorde to be fitted with modern day leather seats in 1993. Last Concorde ever to fly – on November 26, 2003, from Heathrow to Filton.

A wonder of innovation and a 20th century icon – Concorde pushed the boundaries of speed, technology and luxury.

The magnificent white bird, travelling at twice the speed of sound between London, Paris and New York, represented the pinnacle of commercial air travel.

When it first took to the skies in 1969 its systems were the most refined and complex ever seen, its pointed nose, slender fuselage and delta wing gave it the appearance of an arrow pointed at the horizon and it went faster than a rifle bullet.

Concorde's passengers were heads of state, royalty, pop stars, millionaires and those so caught up in the dream of supersonic flight that they were willing to part with the enormous cost of a ticket for the greatest airliner ever made.

Concorde: Supersonic Speedbird – The Full Story gives a complete account of this incredible aircraft.

By Bernard Bale, with Dan Sharp
Foreword by Captain Mike Bannister

ISBN: 978-1-909128-23-1 £7.99

00799 >

9 781909 128231